Write to the Point

BILL STOTT

Write to the Point

AND FEEL BETTER
ABOUT YOUR WRITING

ANCHOR PRESS/DOUBLEDAY
GARDEN CITY, NEW YORK
1984

ISBN: 0-385-19371-8
Copyright © 1984 by Bill Stott
All Rights Reserved
Printed in the United States of America
First Edition

Library of Congress Cataloging in Publication Data

Stott, Bill, 1940–
  Write to the point.

  Includes index.
  1. English language—Rhetoric. 2. English language—Grammar—1950–   .
I. Title.
PE1408.S7665   1984   808'.042   83-24370

For Student X
and my other students and teachers

Contents

Write to the Point

1
WHAT COUNTS IN WRITING

You have opened the book and are reading its first sentence. But is it a book for you?

Yes, if you are insecure about your writing. Maybe you are insecure because you

- are a beginning writer
- fear you are a bad writer
- realize you never learned how to write.

Whatever the reason, this book means to help.

It also means to help if insecurity led you to an "academic" way of writing you now find stilted and empty and hard to shake.

This book will tell you how to write strong, correct sentences. It will tell you how to organize your writing. Most important, it will tell you how to write worthwhile stuff.

I hope you like it.

If you are insecure about your writing, you know it. You sit down to write with a knot in your stomach and a few clanky thoughts in your head. You have to strain to put your thoughts in words and then your words in sentences. You write in a fog of uncertainty, wondering whether you are handling the subject you're supposed to, whether you have organized your thoughts, whether your writing is correct and interesting. Above all, as you stare at the sentences you've written, you wonder whether they say what you mean them to. You still aren't sure when you give your writing to someone else to read.

When it comes back, you hesitate to look at it. You think, "Maybe they've found out." And sometimes they have. A conscientious reader has filled the margins with comments: trite, redundant, tone, trans, awk, why are you telling me this? diction, parallel construction, punc, overwritten, frag, nonsense, thud.

You think, "What do they want? What am I going to do?"

Hang on: I'm going to tell you. You and I are going to rethink nonfiction writing from square one.

First Things First

The first thing you need is encouragement. I think we English teachers have made many mistakes in trying to teach you to write. In this book I'm going to discuss these mistakes. Here is the biggest one: we have diminished your confidence that you can say what you mean to say.

The following paper was written by a student in a second-semester freshman English composition course I taught last year. Students were asked to write a paper beginning "The chief problem I have with my writing is . . ." or "The chief problems I have with my writing are . . ."

WHAT BOTHERS ME ABOUT WRITING

The chief problem I have with writing is not being able to put down in words exactly what my mind is thinking. It has become such a problem that I get parenoid whenever I have to write a paper. In fact, I don't even enjoy writing anymore, instead, it seems more of a hassle.

I wasn't always like this. I enjoyed writing when I was younger and in high school, but ever since my first semester of Freshman English (which was last semester), I've obtained this terrible feeling towards writing papers. I guess it all came about because of the professor I had and what he had to say about my papers that brought my present situation on. It seemed as though whatever I wrote, he had no positive comments about it and all negative ones. This made me lose confidence in my writing ability and it made me feel like I did not know how to write at all.

So now, whenever I begin writing a paper I do not write what comes to my mind, but instead am first concerned with the sentence structure, word choice, organization, content, whether it is coherent, or whatever other rules are involved with English writing. I realize this is important to consider, but it has kept me from writing what and how I feel. I feel as if I have been smothering myself with all of these rules and regulations *before* I write so that I can not write. In fact, I feel like it is not even me who is writing the paper. It is like I have lost my own creativity and originality because of this parenoid feeling.

I do not like not being able to enjoy writing, because it is such a good way to express one's self. In fact, this is the first paper in which I have expressed myself in exactly the way I feel. I felt very relaxed because I said what I had to say and did not concern myself with the "rules" of English writing.

I thank you very much, professor Stott for allowing us to write this paper, because I can say for myself that it took a load off my mind and maybe I can begin to enjoy writing again.

I love this paper. I have to tell you that right off.

The paper is printed here just the way Student X wrote it, and it has faults. It doesn't obey all the rules X complains about. I've showed the paper to various people and been interested in their reactions. If I say to them, "Hey, would you read this paper? I love it," they read it and say they like it too. But if I don't tell them how I feel about it, they read it and start talking about its problems. One woman said, "Every freshman tries that—once," pointing to a lapse of taste in the paper. I left a copy of the paper for a composition-teaching colleague to read. It came back with words circled and a rash of abbreviated corrections down its side.

Not the right response, but the response most people have.

When I read Student X's paper for the first time, I read it as I read all student papers: pen in hand, making harassing noises in the margin.

And that is the chief thing I want to complain about in this book.

Faults

But what about you? Reading X's paper, were you struck by its faults? Do you expect this book to explain and criticize them? Do you think X should be punished for misspelling *paranoid?* How much? (Insecure writers are often hard on other writers. It's a way of feeling one-up.) Or are you frankly unsure what the paper's problems are? Are you waiting for me to tell you?

You put me in an awkward position. You see, I want to encourage your writing by arguing that Student X's point of view is the one to have. X suggests that saying what he wants to is more important than correctness, organization, word choice, and the like. I agree. I think the importance of correctness especially has been exaggerated. Most writing errors don't matter much. X's paper has faults, but they don't do the paper any real harm.

Let's forget about faults for now. Because you have a right to know what I think the faults in X's paper are, I will put an appendix at the end of the book reprinting the paper and discussing the faults I consider worth mention. You may read the appendix now if you want (it begins on page 202), but I hope you won't. I hope you won't for the same reason that I am not going to talk about the faults here. To talk about them here would be to use the self-protective method habitual to us English teachers and deal first with a paper's weaknesses rather than its strengths. English teachers are such timid souls we like to prove we recognize "correct" writing before we pay attention to what the writing says.

That's what I'm doing now! Student X says that too much

emphasis on the rules of English keeps him from saying what he wants; I respond by telling you his paper has faults. Sad.

I'm going to read the paper again.

A Second Try

It is an honest and heartfelt paper. It says something important in a convincing way. Reading it, *absorbing* its meaning, makes criticism of its faults seem beside the point.

The paper uses the tactic of intentional self-contradiction. It says one thing and does (and thus proves) another. Student X says he has trouble "writing what and how I feel" while excellently writing what and how he feels. His paper has a tone of joy, liberation, and amazement ("Look what I'm doing: I'm *saying* it!"), which is very different from the tone of most papers I got from this assignment. Here are the first three paragraphs of Student Y's paper:

MY WRITING

The chief problem I have with my writing is being able to say what I want to say. When I begin to write I feel like my mind is all mixed up inside. No words will come to mind. If I were to write a letter or a journal my writing would improve 100%. I feel more relaxed. I make writing more difficult than it really is because I think and try too hard to express myself in proper words. In my younger days I hated to read. Reading helps to enlarge one's vocabulary, therefore my vocabulary is poor along with my word choice.

Choosing the correct word or phrases is a big problem in my writing. I will sit for thirty minutes thinking of one word. I have no variety of words. Last semester, my English teacher pointed out all the linking verbs I used in one paper. I had two action verbs and about seven linking verbs. When I was a junior in high school my teacher told me I used elementary words in my paper.

All these critics helped me to be aware of my writing, but also lowered my confidence. Lacking confidence is also a problem I have. I am unsure of myself and my ability to write. I hope this year I gain some confidence.

Student Y's paper is a heartbreaker. Y had been kicked so often that he had lost the will to fight. He had given up hope of writing in a way acceptable to his English teachers (which was okay) or to himself (which was not).

I couldn't reach Y. I tried to tell him the teachers had been wrong, that richness of vocabulary, love of reading, active and passive verbs (even seven linking verbs in a row) weren't what mattered. But he had learned from stricter masters than I what his writing was worth (zilch), and he didn't listen.

Confession Time

No wonder the paper I go back to is X's. I said insecure writers need encouragement. The truth is most writers need encouragement. For most people writing is painful work. I've written four books, two of which have been published, and I'm not sure there is a page I have enjoyed writing. There are sentences I've enjoyed because they came easily and fit well with what I had written before. There are some paragraphs. But pages? I enjoy *thinking* about writing them beforehand, and revising and polishing them later, and having—finally!—written them. But not actually writing them. I wrote the early chapters of my dissertation, which became my first book, in a despair I am glad almost to forget. I promised myself that if I finished the dissertation I would tell my students of the mood in which it was written, hoping thus to make them realize that writing is tough for other people too. Certainly I have never sat down to write, even this unburdening paragraph, when I wouldn't rather have been doing something else.

But I find that Student X's paper, which I assigned to encourage him, encourages me. It makes me feel good. It helps me have the guts to write this book, which I very much want to write but which (1) may mislead a few readers (though in a different way from most composition teaching), (2) will make some English teachers chuckle, and (3) looks from where I stand, having written its first six pages, impossible to organize.

It *can* be organized, of course. But there isn't one "right" way to do it. It can be organized many different ways because I don't have just one point I want to make. I have many things to say, and none of them seems logically to come first. If I could do it, I would say everything at the same time.

In such a case I have come to think the best thing to do is write to the point: say immediately what you want to say most, even if it doesn't "come first." There are three reasons for doing this. First, you will then have said it, even if nothing else gets said. Second, your readers will then have read it, even if they read no more. Third, having said it, you are likely to have to say something more, because you will have to explain and justify what you chose to say.

The Message

So . . . I take a big breath and I write what I want most to tell you:

Reader, I want you to write better, and in this book I will do my best to tell you how. But as much as I want you to write better, I want you to *feel* better about your writing.

Student X concluded his paper, ". . . maybe I can begin to enjoy writing again." After these words I wrote, "Wonderful. I hope so." I then wrote a general comment on the paper:

That's very encouraging and even touching to me, Mr. X. And you have expressed yourself well. I hope you'll remember this paper—or, better, the *feeling* you had writing it and finishing it—when you have other things to write in our course, other courses, and for the rest of your life. If you aren't saying what you really want to, something's wrong. If a teacher doesn't want you to, something's wrong with him or her.

I tried to make this point to X's class. Most of its students had shown a weak command of English in their College Boards and in a preliminary English department test. I said to them something like the following:

Many of you have trouble writing correct English. You should work to improve your writing. But don't let your difficulties with

English keep you from saying what you want to say. Be bold. Don't be intimidated by your teachers. Certainly don't be intimidated by English. It's your language too—the teachers don't own it. If you find after working at it that you still don't write well, don't let this keep you from writing what you want to write.

Bad Writing

I realize now there are stronger ways to make this point. Let me ask you a question. What do we mean when we say a paper is badly written?

You know what bad writing is, I know what bad writing is, everybody knows what it is. But so far as I know there is no definition of it. I've tried to come up with one. It says the obvious—but I think we need to have it said.

When we say something is badly written, we mean either

1. it is poorly conceived or argued. That is:
- it doesn't make clear what it is trying to say, what its point is, what it's about (if it's about anything: frequently bad writing isn't)
- its point is trivial or obvious or both
- it doesn't give the detail, the concrete examples, needed to support its point
- it doesn't follow commonsense logic, or

2. its words and sentences have faults of
- coherence
- taste
- correctness, or

3. it has the weaknesses of both 1 and 2.

What I was trying to tell Student X and his class, and what I tell you now, reader, is that there are two kinds of bad writing: type 1 and type 2. The type 2 kind of bad writing is unfortunate and enfeebling, but not ruinous. You can be a bad writer of the type 2 sort and still be a good writer. And if you can't be a really good writer, that's the kind of bad writer to be, a type 2, a good (content) bad (form) writer.

Proper writing isn't of primary importance. What is of primary importance is what the writing says.

Good Bad Writing

There are good bad writers everywhere. They know that the purpose of communication is to say something.

One such man was in my office about a month ago. He works for a publishing company, traveling the Southwest explaining their textbooks to college teachers and scouting writers for future books. He is zooming up the corporate ladder. He and I talked about the teaching of composition, and I said I thought we English teachers were doing our students no favor when we landed on them hard for writing faults. "The students tune out. They give up," I said. "And it isn't the faults that really matter."

The publisher's representative agreed and then volunteered that he had to write many reports for his company and couldn't punctuate. "Sounds crazy," he said, smiling and giving a shrug. "I was a humanities major. I *tried*. I just never got it. I don't know where to put the commas—I put too many."

I asked him how he wrote the reports.

"I've got a secretary who can punctuate. Thank God! I put in commas and she takes them out."

Usually a good bad writer's problems are more serious than punctuation. Before I became a teacher I spent three years with the U.S. foreign service in Africa doing cultural affairs work. One of my bosses, a woman of high rank in the service, had difficulty writing two consecutive sentences. You might think this is a fatal handicap for one who was a communicator. Not at all. My boss was too clever, had too many ideas, to shut up. She wrote as politicians do. That is, she roughed out what she wanted to say for her secretary. The secretary, like a speechwriter, put what the boss said into written form. (The secretary was Cameroonian, English her fourth language. She wrote better in her fourth language than our boss did in her first.) My boss went over what the secretary wrote, making corrections with a felt-tip pen when the secretary had muffed an idiom or reversed what the boss meant to say. The prose that resulted wasn't brilliant, but it got the boss' sometimes brilliant ideas across. Because the secretary wasn't an American citizen, she wasn't allowed to read classified messages and couldn't collaborate in their composition. So when my boss had to send such messages, she wrote them herself—but always sent telegrams. She had no trouble composing a telegram because telegrams aren't writing, they are *lists*. A telegram doesn't need to be organized. Its language needn't flow. One thing is said, then another, then another. Then it stops.

Much of the world works the way my boss did with her secretary: those who have something to say rely on others' help in writing it up. Prominent people tell their stories through ghosts or press agents. Big-league scientists have research staffs, one member of which isn't a scientist but a word-person there to make sure reports and grant applications are coherently written. I know such a person, an ex-history teacher who got fed up with the Mickey Mouse rules at a suburban college. She now counsels scientists thirty years her senior on their prose. Her boss, a zoologist, backed her up in a staff memo that concluded: "I don't care how good the project is. If nobody can understand it, it's NO good." She wrote the memo for him.

Even professional writers require help, sometimes lots of it. Theodore Dreiser, a *great* bad writer, had a stable of confidants who tried to smooth what he wrote into polite language (they succeeded too well: his writing is worst when it tries to be best). I have heard that one of our most successful writers today has a similar stable of researchers and secretaries. Nevertheless, when he presents his publisher with a new manuscript, a senior editor spends two months working on it—"Englishing it," they say in the trade.

The truth is, nearly everybody needs help with their writing. That's why there are editors. A friend of mine is a lawyer for a broadcasting network in New York. She spends part of her time counseling affiliated stations with cases coming to trial. The stations have local lawyers working on the cases long before she appears. These lawyers naturally resent the intrusion of a New York lawyer. Because they do, they prepare the cases well. My friend says their legal briefs are so crammed with precedents she couldn't get another one in with a plunger. However, she says the local lawyers tend to overlook one thing. Information itself doesn't make a case: information must be intelligibly written up. My friend sees her role as playing the country bumpkin English teacher, thus forcing the locals to play the sharpie lawyers. She reads what they have written and then begins pointing at sentences and saying, "What does this mean?" When told, she says, "Oh, of course! I thought it meant what it said." My friend then helps them rewrite the briefs.

A Protest

But you have a protest you want to make. You say this isn't what you have been told. You have been told that people who don't write clear, correct English aren't thinking clearly and therefore can't have much of value to say.

I know the argument. It is what I was told and what I used to tell my students. I don't think it's true.

I gave a 100-question test on grammar, syntax, sentence structure, punctuation, diction, and organization to the twenty-five students in Student X's class. The two students who got the worst scores (low sixties) were among the most interesting essay writers in the class—consistent A—, B. The two students who got the highest scores (low nineties) wrote mediocre themes, B—, C. And my class wasn't peculiar in this. The Educational Testing Service, the company that puts out the College Boards and the Graduate Record Exam, has done studies that found the same thing: there seems to be no correlation between those who write correctly and those who write usefully.

But (you answer) some people do *both*. They have something to say and they know how to write good English. How about them? Where are they?

They—the good good writers—are where they have always been: few and far between. They are a small percentage of the population. Less than 10 percent, I'm sure. Too few to keep a modern economy running.

I am now going to do a little historical speculation. First, some facts. In the old days an education meant something because few people got one. We Americans pride ourselves on our tradition of free public schooling, but guess what percentage of our young people got through high school at the turn of the century. Less than 10 percent—6.3 percent: 63 out of every 1,000 youngsters. (Less than 2 percent got through college: 19 out of 1,000 people.)

Now the speculation. Let's say for the sake of argument that in 1900 all the high school and college graduates in America wrote good English. I know this isn't true because I've read newspapers of the time, and run-of-the-mill published writing then was much sloppier than today—but let that pass. We will assume that educated people then wrote competently. They did so (isn't it plain?) because nearly all the incompetent writers had been removed from the educational system. Somewhere along the line they were found out and flunked out.* Small wonder educated people wrote good English: those who didn't write good English weren't educated.

I let the cat out of the bag. Did you notice? In the last sentences of the preceding paragraph. I knew I was going to do it sometime. I meant to do it, but I hoped it would come later, when you trusted me more and were more confident in your potential as a writer. Well . . . bad news has a way of not being put off.

Two paragraphs back is a paragraph of speculation ("Now

---

* They flunked in droves. Each year about 20 percent of each class flunked. As late as 1910 only half of school-age children made it through eighth grade. See Daniel P. and Lauren N. Resnick, "The Nature of Literacy: An Historical Exploration," *Harvard Educational Review,* August 1979, p. 382.

This is a typical bottom-of-the-page footnote, our first. It gives bibliographical and supplemental information. We will discuss footnotes later.

the speculation," it begins). I said the speculation was going to be historical, and so it is down to the paragraph's last sentences. Then the historical gets mixed with another sort of speculation, which has to be called psychological. What I imply in those sentences is that some people are bad writers despite efforts to educate them. I come near implying that some people are inherently bad writers.

I regret to say I think this may be true. We don't yet know much about the human brain, but we do know—in fact, have always known—that some people are gifted in ways other people are not. Some people have superior eye-muscle coordination, others do mathematics well, others build engines, others draw, others tell stories. Similarly some of us may be born with the aptitude for learning to write smoothly, clearly, perhaps even correctly. Some of us may have the gift of writing, and some of us not.

One thing that makes me think this is my experience teaching writing. For more than a decade I coached the brightest bad writers in my courses, maybe thirty undergraduate and graduate students whose comments in class were full of provocative ideas. I went through their papers with them, explaining where they got off track, how their arguments ought to go, and ways that each paragraph and, ideally, each sentence in each paragraph could carry it forward. The students watched and gave appropriate responses to questions I put them. They nodded and said they understood, their eyes sometimes moist with discovery. Their subsequent papers were little improved, if at all.

There were three exceptions. Three students actually learned to write better. Their writing had been unfocused and pretentious—though with, I remember, oddly few faults. When I took each of them through one of their papers, showing how it needed to be tighter and more forceful, they, like the other students, said they understood what I was getting at. Unlike the other students, though, they were then able to transfer this understanding to their writing. The next paper each of them wrote was markedly different. It didn't waffle about. It wasn't, like most of what college students (and their teachers) write, self-protective *non*writing. It had cohesion and purpose.

Were the three students more intelligent than the other bad writers I coached? No: if anything, less than the average. Good writers, as proverbial wisdom has it, can be rather dull people. And the three *were* good writers—bad only because they hadn't been told what worked in their writing and what didn't. Once told, they knew what to do. As for the other bad writers, it didn't seem to matter how often they were told: they didn't get the hang of putting a sentence together, building a paper, ending a paragraph.

One student tried to write as her mind moved, virtual stream of consciousness, never stopping for transitions. I told her again and again to slow down, that she was running away from her reader. (Later on, reader, I'll try to slow you down.) She wasn't slowed. I couldn't even get her to straighten out her apostrophes. For three months I jumped up and down in the margin of her papers. The semester ended and she was still writing—typing!—"did'nt" (sometimes three times a page: she thought it correct) and "womens' rights" (or "womens rights") and (a favorite sentence) "Cheerleaders and Kick Team's copying the Rangerette type wiggle and jiggle for the masculine benefit." She used "it's" and "its" interchangeably—but then so many students do this that I've lost the feel for which is right where, and have to stop and think. My student, like a considerable percentage of her generation, wants to go into broadcast journalism. She has things to say and the personality to get people to listen. Hell or high water, she'll make a career of it. A fine example of a good (content) bad (form) writer.

My Mistake

Thinking it over now, I realize I was dumb to make so much of her apostrophes. She wasn't ready to learn to write correctly. Like many freshmen, she was too excited by all that was happening to her. Later on she might have been able to listen better. According to composition-critic Janet Emig, my fussing about apostrophes was, like most of what English teachers do, "essentially a neurotic activity." It made me feel better, but it did the student no good. "There is little evidence," Emig says, "that the persistent pointing out of errors in student themes leads to the elimination of these errors, yet teachers spend much of their energy in this futile and unrewarding exercise."*

I realize also that I now give different advice than I used to —more cynical advice. Now I'd tell the student with apostrophe problems to get someone to clean up her papers before she let them out of the house. *Pay* someone if necessary. But what I want to insist upon is that she and the other bad writers I coached were regularly writing good stuff. Which means, I see now, that my psychological speculation has two parts.

I speculate (1) that people may be born to write well or badly and (2) that writing well or badly has nothing to do with having something to say. Until a couple of days ago I had assumed, without much caring, that psychologists would pooh-pooh these ideas. But I spoke then with a psychologist friend, David Hovland, who told me some psychologists would find my ideas plausible. Most psychologists now believe that intelligence—the power so uncertainly measured by IQ tests—has a number of (perhaps many) components. The psychologist J. P. Guilford has argued that intelligence is made up of at least a hundred and twenty "unique intellectual abilities," two of which he described in a way similar to mine.** Guilford called the abilities "fluency" and "creativity" and did experiments that demonstrated that people of high fluency, who express themselves easily and well, are not necessarily people of high creativity who come up with unusual formulations, new ideas. And vice versa: people of high

* Janet Emig, *The Composition Process of Twelfth Graders,* National Council of Teacher of English Research Report no. 13, Urbana, Ill., 1971, pp. 99.

** J. P. Guilford, *The Nature of Human Intelligence,* New York, 1967, p. 465. Guilford's book is tough for those, like me, who haven't learned psychometrics. A nonstatistical description of his theory of the "structure of intellect" is in R. J. Herrnstein, *I.Q. in the Meritocracy,* Boston, 1973, pp. 98–103.

creativity don't necessarily have high fluency. There is only a low correlation between fluency and creativity: to be high or low in one doesn't mean you will be high or low in the other. Many psychologists now think, as one of them says, that there is "little relationship between creativity and IQ scores."* Some of them would presumably accept my corollary thesis: that a person can be a good bad writer and write well (creatively) without writing well (fluently).

Let's assume that Guilford as I understand him is right: fluency and creativity are separate, largely unrelated components of intelligence. What implication does this have for the teaching of writing?

People are supposed to learn to write in school and college. They have high and medium and low fluency and creativity. Those charged with teaching them to write—English teachers like me—are generally people of high fluency. It is appropriate that we be English teachers, as that we be secretaries, journalists, admen, and so on: we love language and beautiful things made of it. It is reasonable that we teach writing: you learn to play golf from someone who plays competent golf. We are not professionals, but most of us hope someday "to write"—by which we mean, of course, write for publication. Our influence on students of high fluency is positive. They can copy what we say and do.

But consider our influence on students of low fluency—on you, reader, if you are a bad writer. What do we do for you? We set you unreachable goals. We make writing seem more difficult than it is. We encourage you to write in a language that is stilted, insincere, and too complex for you to handle easily. If a recent study is correct, we give higher marks to pompously written papers than to simply written ones *saying the same thing.*** When you have trouble and come to us for

* Malcolm R. Westcott, quoted in Frank Riessman, "The Hidden IQ," in Alan Gartner and others, editors, *The New Assault on Equality: IQ and Social Stratification,* New York, 1973, p. 219.

** See Rosemary L. Hake and Joseph M. Williams, "Style and Its Consequences," *College English,* September 1981, pp. 433–51. Maybe Student X was right to be paranoid.

guidance, we say you need a bigger vocabulary (but why? what has that to do with writing?) or a *better* style or "more" style (whatever that means). Or we tell you: read good writing—novels, plays, essays, Hawthorne, Shaw, Hemingway, Nabokov. (As well tell people who want to housebreak a dog that they will learn to do it by watching a lion tamer's act.) Finally, and worst of all, when you have failed to be a competent writer by our standards, we let you know it: we take away your confidence in your ability to express yourself.

That isn't the only way we mislead you. We overemphasize writing, yes—but we also underemphasize what writing is about. We punish low fluency and don't adequately reward high creativity. There are at least three reasons for this.

First, as I said, we have been told that fluency and creativity go hand in hand—that people with things to say write capably. It ain't necessarily so.

Second, we are timid about grading creativity. It is easier and, we tell ourselves, less subjective to grade writing faults, particularly those faults of correctness and taste that go by the name of grammar. "It's no accident that so much attention is paid to grammar in the teaching of writing," says Peter Elbow, a teacher of writing. "Grammar is the one part of writing that *can* be straightforwardly taught."* I agree it is difficult to measure a person's creativity in general (we leave such tasks to the psychologists), but it isn't hard to judge a specific paper's creativity—its originality and usefulness. Teachers who say they can't do it—indeed, don't automatically do it, if only to themselves, when reading a student's paper and every other piece of writing—are fibbing.

Third, most of us English teachers aren't very creative. That's why we are English teachers rather than the writers we probably hoped to be. Something brilliant we may disregard out of lack of practice and, perhaps, envy.

Enough of our defects. You knew them already. If you're a bad writer, you realized long ago that English teachers had it in for you. You learned what to expect from us: criticism and

* Peter Elbow, *Writing Without Teachers*, New York, 1973, p. 138.

indifference. (And such *indifferent* criticism. As if thin general-izations—"awkward word choice," "unfocused argument," "too poetic and elliptical"—were all you needed!) But now the good news. What we think of you and your writing doesn't matter much. We may be of no help, but these days we can't do real harm. As you yourself prove, one doesn't have to write with confidence or skill to get through school and college. If nonfluent writers used to be elbowed out of academe, now they stay in. Everybody stays in. Our social ideals and our economic well-being demand it.

And because so many bad writers now receive an educa-tion, some worrywarts tell us there is a "literacy crisis." I disagree.* Many bright people who have trouble writing are now going to college—that's all. The worrywarts assume that bright, educated people are always proficient writers, and this isn't true. The 1950s are looked back upon as a golden age in American higher education. I went to college then at a First-Class Eastern Private University (Yale). The college told us, for the alumni's overhearing, that we were the country's fu-ture leaders, our year's top 2 percent (or 5 percent—either number was acceptable), bla bla bla. Because I wanted to be a writer, I paid attention to how my fellow students wrote and what teachers said about it. The year I graduated, Yale gave me a fellowship to teach freshman composition for a year, which I gladly did. The next year I graded the papers of juniors and seniors at an Equally First-Class Western Private University (Stanford). My classmates and the students whose papers I graded at Yale and Stanford wrote with the same contortion of language, pomposity, sloppiness, and fear I see in student papers today at a State University of the Aspiring Second Class (the University of Texas at Austin). Despite my efforts, or because of them, bad writers left my charge, then as now, feeling insecure about their ability to write. Justifi-ably so.

* There *is* a literacy problem in America. We have a higher percentage of adults who can't read than most industrialized countries. This is more than regrettable, it is shameful. But we have lived with the problem a long time, and it is not, I think, a crisis. Anyhow, this isn't the "literacy crisis" the worrywarts talk about in the media.

There isn't a literacy crisis. Or, what is to say the same thing, a literacy crisis is always with us. Such a crisis happens anytime somebody picks up a pencil and tries to write something new and worthwhile. But this sort of day-to-day, one-on-one confrontation with language doesn't interest the worrywarts. They are exercised by a Social Problem. What alarms them is the wasteful spectacle of a postindustrial, upwardly mobile, fairly democratic, market-oriented technocracy preparing and half-preparing as many people as possible for the society's essential work—endless innovation, most of it worthless—and giving its work and rewards to the lucky and the best.

For who are the best? Can there be any doubt? The fluent among us are handy, but it's not they. Neither is it the well educated, though they are the worrywarts' favorites. No, it's the creative people, who can rise without pedigree from the least auspicious places—the "vinyl depths," in the happy phrase of journalist Tom Wolfe. The creative people make the difference, and not just those who happen to write smoothly: those whose writing is rough (and you have lots of company, reader) but who come up with notions that make the rest of us pause, the spoon on the way to our lips.

2

HOW TO FIND
SOMETHING TO SAY

The point we have been making is that it's okay to be a bad writer if you have something to say. We will now ask how you get something to say—how you write creatively.

You choose a worthwhile subject, of course. But what is a worthwhile subject? That's the important question because the subject of a piece of writing determines much of its value.

How much? Well, it's foolish to put a number on such things, but trying to wake up a class of students, I have sometimes done it. I've said that the subject—by which I mean what is said, the content, the "point"—is 75 percent of a piece of nonfiction writing. "And the other 25 percent?" you ask. Most of it, 15 or 20 percent, is the organization, the order in which the subject is given. The rest, 10 percent or less, is the writing itself.

I realize that many of the great writers would disagree with me. They are on record as believing that what counts in writing, ultimately, is style. The high priest of this view is the French novelist Gustave Flaubert, who used to tell his friends, "What I'd like to write is a book about nothing, a book unrelated to anything outside itself, which would stand on its own by the internal strength of its style, just as the earth holds itself in space without any support, a book that would have almost no subject or an almost invisible subject, if such a thing were possible."

Is there any way to answer Flaubert? Sure, dozens of ways, some of them polite. Here are four:

1. M. Flaubert, you may be correct that style ultimately determines the value of a piece of writing. But some of us don't aspire to be "ultimate" writers. We just want to write something that does a useful job now.
2. You wanted to write fiction. We want to write nonfiction. The requirements for the two sorts of writing may be different. However, monsieur, you must admit that
3. there are great fiction writers who disagree with you about the preeminence of style. Tolstoy, for example. Dickens and Dostoevsky. Melville and George Eliot. Balzac. (FLAUBERT: "What a genius Balzac would have been had he known how to write!")
4. In this regard it is interesting to note that although you eulogize the absence of subject in a fiction, the book you are best remembered for, *Madame Bovary,* is full of subject. It's about romantic dreams, a bad marriage, class antagonism, adultery, despair, and suicide. (FLAUBERT: "When I wrote about Emma Bovary's poisoning herself, I had the *taste of arsenic* so strongly in my mouth, I got poisoned. I gave myself two bouts of indigestion, one after the other—real indigestion which made me vomit up my whole dinner.")

But the best answer to Flaubert was given by one of his friends, the writer George Sand. She wrote him: "You care for nothing but the well-made sentence. It is something—but it's only something. It isn't the whole of the art of writing: it isn't even half. It's a quarter at most, and when the other three quarters are good, people overlook the one that isn't."

That's exactly my view—the three-quarter view, we could call it. If you write superbly, as Flaubert did, maybe you can write about nothing. But if you merely write well or less than

well, you need to have something good to say. And if you
have something good to say, you won't need to write well. If
you write about something important from an original point
of view (as, say, the philosopher Hegel did), you will be read
with interest, even if you write miserably (as Hegel did).

But to speak of Hegel makes the case too easy. Consider
this instead. Most of us read a newspaper every day. Why?
Not because of the quality of the writing. No: because it's
full of things we want to know about.

So must your writing be.

But how? *How?*

We're back to the crucial question.

What We Read For

But maybe we have an answer for it too. Think about that
daily paper. Why do we read it—or listen to the radio and
TV news? Because they tell us things we hadn't known. They
tell us "news."

That's one way of saying what worthwhile writing does. It
gives news. It informs its readers. It tells us what we hadn't
known or hadn't adequately understood before. It says something original, something useful, something that needs to be
said in a certain context.

The context matters enormously. Student X's paper (page
2) argued that teachers who severely criticize writing faults
may inhibit their students, causing them to write worse. As I
told you (page 5), I think the paper "says something important in a convincing way." But I don't claim for a moment
that the paper said anything that hadn't been said before. No
doubt what it said had been written hundreds of times and
thought millions more. The paper made its point in a touching and hopeful way, I felt, and that's why I decided to use it
in this book.

But that's not the reason I praised the paper in class, read it
aloud, and gave it an A. I did these things because Student
X's paper said something that hadn't been said *there* before.
In the context of the class it *was* original. No one else had put

the argument forward in a paper or in class discussion—not even, I regret to say, the teacher. For the class the paper had news value. It said something that needed to be said.

After hearing X's paper two students wrote papers saying the same thing. Their papers were written in a different context from X's. Their central point was no longer news. X's paper had brought the point to the class' attention, and we had discussed it. Not only was it no longer news, it had become, in the context of the class, a given, *obvious,* part of the furniture.

Does this mean the other students shouldn't have written on the topic? No, but in writing on it they should have taken account of the changed context. That is, they should have said in their papers that they were writing about the subject because of X's paper and then done something new with X's argument. They could have analyzed it, modified it, "refuted" it, or demonstrated it in a fresh way (by, for example, referring to their own experience) and thus "proved" it. Neither student did this. Neither had an original point to make. Their papers got C's.

Everything is written in a context. It is written at a certain time, for a certain purpose, and for someone or some group of people. To write something new and useful, you must know the context, because you have to know what is already known so you can *work against it* in your writing. When you write you must ask yourself, "Who am I writing for? What do they know about the topic? What do they *think* they know? What can I tell them that's different but still plausible? How can I teach them a thing or two?"

The answer will depend on the context.

Context

The context of a piece of writing is either

> serious or frivolous
> public or personal
> formal or casual

student or poststudent
institutional or independent

and so on and on through countless other either-ors. This book is not concerned with writing done in contexts that are frivolous or personal because I think such writing should be done any way the writer pleases. This book is concerned with serious, if often lighthearted, nonfiction writing, formal or casual, done for strangers to read—hence, public—in both student and poststudent, institutional and independent contexts.

The book itself is written in the poststudent context, by which I mean it isn't done for a class, a teacher, a grade, or a degree. It isn't written institutionally, for the approval of a boss or organization or authority. As I will point out when we discuss tone in Chapter 4, an institutional context strongly affects the form that writing takes. It may also have a restraining effect on the content.

The most important writing occurs in the poststudent context. This is because (obviously) the most important work is done there. When I was a boy the principal of my elementary school was a Dr. Paul Allen. I once asked my mother if he was a real doctor. She said he wasn't. "He's called Dr. Allen because he has a degree called the doctorate," she said. "How did he get that?" I asked. My mother was in a hurry. We were on the school stairs, I remember, and I was dawdling. She grabbed my hand, saying, "He had a thought nobody had before."

It's not true, of course. There are no totally original thoughts. But it's a way of indicating how high the poststudent writer can aspire. In doing a Ph.D. dissertation, the student, still a student, nonetheless finally escapes the student role: he or she is required to write something that matters to people out in the world—something that is, as academics say, a contribution to knowledge. This demand is implicitly made of all serious writers when they are done being students.

It is made of me, reader, as I write these words. I make it of myself, and you, a sensible person, jealous of your time, make it of me too. I am writing this book because I believe it needs to be written—the best reason to write anything. When I finish the manuscript, I will have to sell it to an editor. The editor will want my assurance, and then the assurance of experts in the teaching of composition, that it will make a useful book and that, although its author was aware of the latest and most accepted thinking in the field, as well as earlier, discarded thinking, he didn't duplicate much of it. I will then sign the publisher's contract, which has a standard clause promising that my work is "original"—different from anything done before.

That's the *post*student context. Students breathe less rarefied air. Until the dissertation they aren't obliged to be contributors to knowledge, but—and here's the point I'm making—they still must be original . . . in their context.

Let's assume for a moment that you are a college student and want to write a paper on the structure of elite groups in America or the Gravedigger's scene in *Hamlet* or democratic socialism or women's rights or twentieth-century learning theories. Being an undergraduate student you are not expected—can't be—to come up with something that has never been said before, something actually "new." It may be that you will come up with something new, but you won't know it and, often, neither will your teacher. Too much has been written on these topics, and most others, for you or anyone without long specialization to read enough to be able to claim that you have written something unprecedented. But you *can* write something unprecedented in the context of what your class has done, what your teacher has told you about the topic, and what you have learned from your research.

You can (we'll talk about how in a minute), but *should* you? This question troubles many students. Is it really wise for them to try to educate their teachers?

Definitely yes. It is a common myth that teachers don't want to learn anything from students and prefer them simply to echo what they have been told. In my years in and around colleges I've known only one teacher of whom this was true: Yvor Winters (1900–68), a professor of English at Stanford.

A bitter old man when I studied with him, Winters thought his literary criticism had been undervalued by the influential critics of his day. Perhaps for this reason he graded students up or down according to whether they accepted his critical views. Even he, though, was interested in novelty; he gave the strongest praise to students who demonstrated the truth of his views *in a new way.*

There are half a million college teachers in America. There are some of Winters' disposition, who really only want to hear their beliefs confirmed. They are less educators than indoctrinators. But such teachers are a small minority, I'm sure. Most teachers are willing to entertain fresh ideas. Some of us are touchingly grateful. You can understand why when you consider our lives, selling more or less the same bill of goods year after year to students who appear to diminish in age, preparation, and interest. What a treat to have a student *think* about what we are saying, improve upon it, find a new way to skin an old cat. What a treat to have someone take our notions seriously enough to criticize and reject them. This is where education begins. There is dialogue. The student says something that surprises the teacher, who stops talking, starts thinking.

If you can't teach your teacher anything, the best thing to do is try another teacher.

Changing Expectations

I have suggested that if you work against the context in which you are writing, you will say something new. This sounds difficult. What does it mean? It means you challenge your readers' expectations. Michael Domjan, a psychologist at the University of Texas, recently published an article on the mood drug lithium. Here is his first sentence: "A commonplace observation is that we live in a drug-dominated society." Domjan challenges our expectations with a single word: commonplace. His sentence tells us what we know— our society uses lots of drugs—*but tells us that we know it:* it is "a commonplace observation." Because Domjan shows us that he knows what we know (or think we know), we are encouraged to believe he may also know things we do not. We think his article may tell us something. We read on.

When you are working against the context, saying something new, don't keep it a secret. Do like Domjan: let your readers know. It's the hope of learning something that keeps us reading. In *The Boys of Summer* Roger Kahn relates the advice that Dick Young, sportswriter for the New York *Daily News,* once gave him on how to write up a baseball game. Said Young:

Your real fan knows the score already. When you got to write the game, the way you do it is: "In yesterday's 3–2 Dodger victory, the most interesting thing that happened was . . ." Get that? Somebody stole two bases. Someone made a horseshit pitch. Dressen [Chuck Dressen, the Dodger manager] made a mistake. Whatever the hell. Not just the score.

Since the readers already know the score, the context of the game, you have to indicate right off that you have news they don't know.

I wanted the students in X's class to see what it felt like to write a paper that worked against the context of what was generally known. I gave them a list of phrases and asked them to use any one to start the first sentence of their next paper for me. Here are two of the first sentences that resulted.

A. One thing few people realize about the new television show, *Mork and Mindy,* is that it is one of the top five most watched television shows in America today.

B. It hasn't been widely recognized that Woody Allen's movie, *Love and Death,* which takes place in early 18th century Russia, implies that society is a big joke.*

---

* Note: both commas in sentence A and the first comma in sentence B are incorrect. They shouldn't be there. This increasingly common fault I discuss in Chapter 5. Note also that *Love and Death* is set in early *nineteenth*-century Russia: Allen is mocking the world described in the great Russian novels, particularly Tolstoy's *War and Peace.* Note finally that this sort of bottom-of-the-page note, signaled by an asterisk (*), gives peripheral information that would clutter up the argument going forward in the main text.

Okay, reader, what's wrong with those sentences? Not grammar-wrong. *Big* Wrong. Let's not beat around the bush. The sentences gyp the reader. They say they are going to say something new, and then each comes forward with a thundering banality. *Mork and Mindy* is popular, Woody Allen's comedies make fun of society, General Washington decided to cross the Delaware. Someone's got to find other facts to keep our eyes open.

Or else they need to claim less. The students who wrote sentences A and B didn't read far enough down my list. They chose from among the first phrases:

1. No one has yet remarked upon . . .
2. It hasn't been widely [or "generally" or "popularly"] recognized that . . .
3. The most interesting [or "fascinating" or "surprising"] fact about . . . is that . . .
4. One thing few people realize about . . . is that . . .

Farther down the list the phrases got softer:

5. People [or "Critics" or "Recent historians" or "British disc jockeys" or *"People Weekly* and *Parade* magazines"] haven't made much of . . . , but . . .
6. It is a commonplace that . . . But . . . [thanks, Mr. Domjan]
7. It hasn't been properly [or "sufficiently" or "adequately" or "well enough"] understood [or "appreciated" or "recognized"] that . . .

Phrase 7 is particularly handy. However cliché your subject, you can claim it hasn't been "properly" understood, and no reasonable person will disagree without hearing you out. "Everybody knows the new television series *Mork and Mindy* is popular. But it hasn't been sufficiently appreciated just how popular it is." The reader accepts the weakened claim and is ready for some proof (which, of course, needs to be adequate).

What I'm saying is only common sense. First, your claims mustn't affront the reader's common sense. (One of Student

X's classmates wrote: "I present a singular, or so it seems, case on the subject of Women's Liberation. Being a female my case is unique." No, it isn't; there are other females in the world.) Second, your claims have to be "proved," demonstrated—a point we will come back to in the next chapter. Having said this, let me make it plain that you should be making claims like those in the seven phrases above. You may think the phrases dull and obvious; you may devise subtler ways of saying the same thing. But if you put a claim like one of these near the start of a paper, it—if anything—will persuade those interested in the subject to keep reading. If your paper goes on to justify the claim, most readers will think the paper worthwhile, even if it is poorly written.

You *must* make claims: that's the point. You must *assert* something. The chief weakness in most writing is lack of purpose, point, thesis, argument. Over and over I find myself writing in the margins of student papers: "What's your thesis?" "Where's your argument?" "What point are you making?" "Why are you telling me this?" Or, at the end of papers, comments such as,

This paper is full of weak assertions like the one that finishes on this page (the movie was interesting, it was enjoyable). When you say something like this you must go on and tell us why and how and why you bother to tell us about it—why, that is, we should be interested in the movie and the entertainment it provides. You must answer the question I ask now that I've read your paper: "The movie was enjoyable—so what?"

Or this, to a woman student who had written on a book about a young woman's paralysis:

A very healthy book to like, but you don't make a case for *why* we should be interested in it. It's nice, it's healthy—but so what? Why do we *need* to read the book? Why did it move you so? (You claim it did.) Was it because—for example—it showed you, as you enter into adulthood, that even fearsome hardship, should it (pray God not) befall you, won't necessarily mean that there wouldn't be happiness in your life?

Or this, to a student who wrote on the movie *Superman:*

You have a clear mind and a good-spirited way. But you have *nothing* but what is obvious and trite to say here. You must either (1) "prove" the obvious in a fresh way, or (2) say something different.

You trample over dozens of themes, but only once, for part of a sentence, do you come close to telling us anything new. You suggest Superman is a type of Christ. That's exactly what a paper should do, Mr. T—say something new, something unobvious, something everybody doesn't realize. But having said something like this (and you don't even say it: you *hint* it), you have then to prove it, point to lots of evidence in the movie showing that we are meant to understand Superman thus. Then you have to explain what the analogy means. Superman is like Christ: so what? So plenty, you've got to say, and explain why the comparison is important.

So What?

"So what?" is the most devastating question a writer, or any creator, can be asked. It is, I admit, both unfair and unanswerable when simply repeated after every response made to it. (That is the method of the nihilist.) But it is an unavoidable question as long as the person to whom it is put hasn't tried to answer it. Far from asking "so what?" too much, I think most of us ask it too little. Were we to ask it more, the list of things we "have" to read and see and do would be wonderfully shorter.

It is surprising that we teachers don't ask "so what?" more —certainly our students ask it all the time behind our backs. The following passage is from the reputable freshman composition textbook I used with Student X's class: Jim W. Corder's *Handbook of Current English* (5th ed., Glenview, Ill., and London, 1978, pp. 358–59).* Corder is discussing "underdeveloped paragraphs" and to do so cites a student paper:

---

* That "(5th ed., Glenview, Ill., and London, 1978, pp. 358–59)" is a footnote imbedded in the text. Such imbedding avoids the necessity of having a bottom-of-the-page footnote like this.

The effect of underdeveloped paragraphs is illustrated by the following student narration of a trip:

Two years ago I took my first trip to Alaska. On this particular voyage there were only forty-five passengers. I learned from the steward that the usual number of weekly passengers ranged from seventy-five to two hundred.

The fruit basket in each cabin was filled daily with apples, oranges, and other kinds of fruit. Since meals were included in the price of the ticket, we could choose anything we wanted from the menu without worrying about the price.

We arrived at our first port, Sitka, on a rainy day. We were told that the ship would be there for about four hours unloading cargo and that we could go ashore if we so desired. After taking a good look at the town, I decided that I would very much prefer to be on board ship.

These paragraphs don't work well because they raise questions that the writer fails to answer. Why were there so few passengers on this trip? (This should be explained in the first paragraph or else not mentioned.) What is the point of the second paragraph, which jumps so abruptly from the introductory statements? the abundance of food? how cheap it was? how much the writer enjoyed it? Some statement is needed at the beginning of this paragraph to link it with the preceding one and to express the main idea ("Because there were so few passengers, we were offered more food than we could eat . . ."). The third paragraph leaves the reader wondering what Sitka looked like, what unpleasant things the writer saw that made him prefer to stay on his ship. Three or four explanatory sentences would have cleared up this point and would have made the paragraph more interesting.

That's all Corder says about the passage. No doubt he could say more about the things that don't hang together and how they could be made to. But he ought to mention the reason they don't. They don't because the student has no theme, no argument to make, no clear subject. As the writer Gertrude Stein said of Oakland, "There's no *there* there." The student doesn't know what he wants to say, and Corder should tell him so—or at least tell us. It's not much use to talk of sentences lacking "interesting" explanatory detail when the sentences aren't saying anything to begin with. We could redo the student's sentences as Corder invites us to, pumping them full of images ("the apples gleamed like mahogany and tasted like sweet sherry"—that sort of thing). It would still be a pointless piece of writing.

Consider a passage closer to my heart. When my uncle George Merrell (1898–1962) retired from the U.S. foreign service in 1952, he went to live on the Spanish island of Mallorca in the Mediterranean. He had written excellent reports on foreign places and politics for the Department of State and now decided to try his hand at writing for *The New Yorker,* a magazine he loved. He wrote a two-thousand-word essay about life on Mallorca and sent it to E. B. White, the writer and *New Yorker* editor, whom he had known when both were students at Cornell. Here is the first paragraph of George's article:

One can find almost any kind of person and any kind of thing in Mallorca. My egg woman who provides large brilliantly white eggs with her crest on them is a Polish countess married to a German. They live with her Polish mother and a Spanish aristocrat who calls himself a Filipino. My cook was born not *sur* but within a stone's throw of the *Pont d'Avignon.* He is married to a girl from Andalusia. My secretary, who has just been baptized and confirmed by the Bishop of Palma, is Chinese, and my masseur is a blind Frenchman who receives a pension from the State of New Jersey and can read pasts and futures through radiation and mummify fish and beefsteaks through the magnetism of his fingers. The most delightful hostess on the Island, who lives in an old mill near Pollensa, is Rumanian. The most interesting figure on the Island, unless it is Robert Graves, who is a wonderful combination of a boy with boundless enthusiasm and a sage with abundant erudition, is an expert horsewoman whose father was Hindu and mother a gypsy. She lived with her mother's tribe for 18 years and was required to have the gypsy's brand erased from her arm with nitric acid when she finally left the tribe.

The New Yorker turned the essay down. I don't know the reason given. Apparently George didn't tell our family and didn't save the letter of rejection.

You have read the first paragraph. Do you have an idea why the article was refused? It doesn't have the problems Corder saw in the Alaskan trip narrative: George's writing hangs together and is crowded with colorful detail. So what's the problem?

So what.

The theme is the problem. It's too weak to justify an article. And it didn't develop into something more complex later on. It was given, whole, in the first sentence: "One can find almost any kind of person and any kind of thing in Mallorca." Well, big deal. Whoever thought you couldn't? Everybody knows you can find many sorts of people just about anywhere. Who needs two thousand words proving that? The essay has a *there* there—but not enough of one.

Nevertheless, it's a promising essay because of the good detail and chuckling tone. George could have used both in articles people would have learned things from—as, for example, about the sort of people who choose expatriate life, the reasons for expatriation, its hardships, its economics, its politics (under Spanish dictator Francisco Franco—*most* interesting). George says later in the essay that Mallorca was known as the poor man's Riviera. He could have compared the ethnic mix, "native" population, standards of decorum, social classes, at the two resorts. White's letter of rejection may have suggested how the article could be improved. I'm sure the letter was as constructive as the rest of his writing. I regret George wasn't more interested in saying anything as a writer. Rejected this once, he never tried to write for publication again.*

* I sent a Xerox of the preceding paragraphs about my uncle George to E. B. White to see whether he had any comment. White kindly replied to my letter and said that, contrary to published reports, he was never a *New Yorker* editor. When he received George's essay, he gave it to someone who made decisions on what the magazine published. Because George was a friend and deserved a personal as well as an institutional response, White thinks he wrote him a letter explaining the reason for the rejection. He doesn't remember the reason but guesses it was what I suggest: the theme was too weak.

You note, reader, that I have not quoted a word of White's letter directly. This is because I haven't the right to do so. Under the "fair use" provisions of the recent (1976) U.S. copyright law one may quote small amounts of published, copyrighted

Or consider something I wrote. My wife and I had been out of touch with the K's, our fairly good friends, for almost ten years. Then, being nearby on business, I tried their old phone number. I got Bob. After some talk I asked how Margaret was, and Bob, taken aback, said, "Didn't you know? She died." She had died four years earlier, in her mid-thirties, of an unstoppable cancer. Once home I sent Bob a note, and he replied with a touching letter about his life. It took me a month, but I answered. Here is the way I started:

Thanks so much for your warm, funny, sad letter. I've been writing little answers to it, little replies, while lying in bed at night and walking down rainy streets. Even now that I have a hard and factual typewriter before me I am not sure that I know what I want to say; in fact I suppose I am sure only that what I want to say can't really *be* said. Which is no doubt why I've taken these weeks to reply: it takes a long while to say what can't be said.

And changing paragraphs doesn't help.

What I wrote here is worse than any other bad writing I quote in this book. Its badness isn't verbal, it's moral. My letter has nothing to say and says that nothing *cutely.* It calls attention to itself—and to me—and away from what had to be the topic: Bob's loss, Margaret's death.

The fault in my letter is the fault we have been talking about: lack of something to say or, here perhaps, the nerve to say it. I tried to overcome the lack by writing "interestingly." Fluent writers are liable to do this: let their *manner* substitute for a subject, replace content with cleverness. (E. B. White

---

prose for instructive purposes without the copyright owner's permission. Only with permission, however, may one quote unpublished writing like White's letter. The letter belongs to me (White sent it to me), but its words belong to him (he wrote them) and are protected by copyright for his lifetime plus fifty years more. I have closely paraphrased his letter here, as I am allowed to do. Of course had I been willing to bother him again, as I was not, I could have asked him for permission to quote the letter directly.

As you note also, this is an asterisked bottom-of-the-page note that runs *beyond* the bottom of the page where it began. No sweat. On this, the subsequent page, the continuing footnote is simply set off from the main text by a line—short or long— from the left margin.

himself is not always exempt from this charge.) A graduate student in a class I taught last year relied too much on her gifts as a writer to put her papers over. Her last paper of the semester was a vague yearning for the "social excitements" of the 1960s. My comment on the paper ended:

The problem is the writing is too good for the little you have to say. You are so talented a writer that you permit yourself to be "cute," to *obviously* polish your words and, more, your locutions ("what's left of the Left" is a good one) till they sparkle so much and *so often* that our eyes are taken off the target and your argument, and on to you, Clever Girl. This is dangerous, I honestly believe, Ms. R. There is too much cleverness in the world, most sensible people think, and too little truth. Let's try to have more truth.

Originality

More truth—and yet the truth cannot be easy or obvious. As the critic Renata Adler has observed, the bitterest words a writer can hear are "What you say is true, but not very interesting." (This is just "so what?" said genteelly.) Readers are not looking for truisms. They are looking—we say it again—for something new.

Originality of content hasn't always been so prized. When William Shakespeare determined to make an immortal name for himself by writing a sonnet sequence, the prestige literary form of his day, he chose to write on the themes the great poets had used: carpe diem, the fragility of flesh versus the permanence of rhyme, passion accumulating and passion spent. He wanted to write on these matters superbly, and often claims in the sonnets to have done so, but he didn't feel the need to find a subject different from his predecessors.

Neither did young John Milton. He was eager for fame ("Fame is the spur that the clear spirit doth raise," he announced) and so wrote a pastoral elegy, a poetic form then in vogue, on the death of a young man he had known at college. Milton made the content of his elegy as much as possible like earlier elegies—Greek, Roman, Italian, French. He called the dead man "Lycidas" (though his name was Edward King), pictured him as a poet-shepherd in an Edenic garden (though he was a teacher-administrator drowned on the crossing to Ireland), and surrounded him with the bric-a-brac of classical convention: muses, nymphs, fountains, fauns, a funeral procession, "pensive" flowers, and heartsick sheep. Milton's readers, all educated people, would have immediately seen what he was up to—but that was the point. He was proving himself a poet by writing a poem like many poems written before but unusually excellent in its language.

This was the traditional view of what good writing did: it provided a memorable statement of conventional material. This view was immortalized in a couplet by the poet Alexander Pope (for whom, we note, the word *wit* meant skill with words):

> True wit is Nature to advantage dressed,
> What oft was thought, but ne'er so well expressed.

As consequence of this view, students used to practice writing by the method called imitation. What they did was rewrite a passage or poem by an author of established worth, borrowing the manner and tone (almost always), the topic (usually), the content (as much as they cared to), even particular metaphors and locutions. They were judged on their writing skill and often by how well they captured the essence of the original work.

There is a good deal to be said for imitation. It develops fluency. It acquaints students with writers of the past. It calms those who fear they have nothing to say. Perhaps it demystifies the writing process—surely a good thing. Furthermore, since the method was part of a classical education and the authors imitated generally wrote in a foreign language, imitation provided a subtle test of a student's grasp of that language.

The drawback of the imitation method—no surprise—is that it doesn't promote originality. But when did originality become so important? This is a question for which no definite answer is possible. Some scholars would want to go all the way back to the invention of writing and written information's displacement of aural knowledge. Others would cite the Renaissance and its new man, little less than an angel. Media-thinker Marshall McLuhan would bring up Gutenberg's movable type.

I think many scholars would put the revolution (it is nothing less) closer to our own time—in the eighteenth century, the age of revolutions. They would point out that whereas Pope's definition of writing belongs to that century's early years (1709, to be exact), by the end of the century a new and different idea of writing was coming to prominence. No longer would poets merely verbalize what oft was thought. Now they sought to express their individual selves, their emotions, their personal experience and unique perceptions. For William Wordsworth, writing in 1800, "Poetry is the spontaneous overflow of powerful feelings." For William Blake, "One Power alone makes a Poet: Imagination, the Divine Vision." A century after Pope, Percy Shelley wrote, "Poets are the unacknowledged legislators of the world"—originators, not clever mouthpieces for what everybody knows. And John Keats boasted, "I never wrote one single line of poetry with the least shadow of public thought."

We have no satisfactory explanation of why this revolution took place. We know it did and the rich name it has been given, Romanticism. We may be still too close to it, too much its heirs, to really comprehend it. Nevertheless, some of its causes are surely

- the philosophies and psychologies of John Locke and Jean Jacques Rousseau
- the American and French revolutions and their propaganda on behalf of individual liberty
- the rise of the novel with its concern for the individual, extreme emotions (particularly in the Gothic novels then popular), and unusual locales and behavior
- the spread of the newspaper and its appetite for the new
- the triumph of science and technology with their bias toward innovation

• the growth of the idea of progress, both for the individual (who could rise in the world) and society (which could make the world better)—progress, the least traditional and most disruptive of ideas.

But why and whenever the rage for originality started, started it has. It is a fact of modern life. And just as we're not going back to traditional methods of farming or to a subsistence economy (though some of us like to pretend we might), so we're not going back to the old standard for writing: what matter how tired the content if the form be good. Imitation has had its day. We now expect even novice writers to see the difference between saying something new and something known.

There's nothing for it, reader: we must live with the living and try to make them lend an ear.

The Question Again

But—for the last time—HOW? What can you write, reader, that will be original, worthwhile, important, interesting?

I don't know. I don't know because I don't know the context in which you are writing. If I knew the context, I might be able to suggest a topic or two. When a student comes up after class and asks me for something to write on, I can occasionally dredge up an idea, since I know what we haven't covered in the course. Usually students don't like my suggestions. They give a sullen nod, say, "Yeah. Thanks," or, if they are bold, admit the topic doesn't interest them. (And why should it? It had some inner urgency for me, not for them.) I then say something like the following: "I'm sorry you're not interested in what I suggest. I'm not much interested in it either. The stuff I *am* interested in I say in class, where, as you may have noticed, I've suggested other topics." Then, if necessary, I repeat parts of an earlier speech I made to the class:

As a teacher I feel I'm responsible for being interested in what I teach. But I don't feel I'm responsible for interesting you. I try to interest you, but if you're not interested that's your business.

The same with paper topics. I don't consider it my responsibility to find one that interests you. I suggest topics that occur to me, but if they don't interest you, too bad.

I think it's your responsibility to find a subject that interests you. Writing is like life in this: salvation is individual. You're the one who has to discover what you think matters greatly.

What I tell my students and my classes I tell you now, reader. Though there is no end of worthwhile subjects, coming up with a worthwhile subject at a given time, in a given context, is usually hard work. This is because imagination, creativity, call it what you will, is always in short supply.

That's part of what I want this book to suggest: how tough it is to do meaningful writing and how most people prevent themselves from doing it *at the start* by choosing a trivial or exhausted subject.

I hope this book encourages your sense of what it means to write something that *needs* to be written. I hope it encourages you to grab hold of a subject where it's alive, with blood throbbing under the skin, not where it's turned to stone and ash.

What should you write on? Here are my suggestions.

• Write on something you care about, something that touches, puzzles, angers, amuses you. Try to do this whether you have the whole world of topics to choose from or must stick to an assigned topic. Write about something that provokes a real response in you. I suggest this for several reasons.

First, if you write on something you care about, you will probably write better. You believe the subject important, so you are likely to want others to agree and feel about it as you do. You may be willing to take time to look at it hard and communicate it well. If you won't do this for a subject you like, when will you?

Second, if you write on something you care about, you

may not care so much what other people think of what you write. The feedback you get, the grade or whatever, will count less because you have the satisfaction of having said something you believe in.

Third, writing on a subject that engages you will almost certainly change your feelings about it: clarify, complicate them—maybe use them up (it's happened). This sort of growth is good in itself and often seeps back into what you write, making it richer. We want to promote this—which leads me to the next point.

· When you write on something you care about, try to make it something you haven't yet entirely made up your mind about. Such a subject gives you the best chance to learn from what you write.

I am convinced many writers actually write better when they don't know beforehand everything they are going to say. It's hard for some of us to get interested in writing if we know a subject so well we see it only the way we know it and can't be surprised into new knowledge. I sometimes think I recognize the writing of people who are not learning as they write. It has a dry, mechanical sound like the muttering of an auctioneer. I wonder if anyone has written an interesting account of the virtues of their religion or a dull account of their search for God.

· When you choose something you care about as a subject, make sure you don't just care about it "in general." Make sure there are particular aspects, people, events, pictures, turns of phrase that strike you and suggest to you things you want to say.

I say this because I know I care about many subjects—pop music, the Fauves, abortion, Northern Ireland, the arms race, the Third World—about which I have nothing particular to say. The trouble with having nothing particular to say is that one's opinions stand forth nakedly as the clichés they are. To bring your opinions alive you need something specific—journalists call it a peg—on which to hang them.

I need a peg here—an example to show you what I mean. Autobiography to the rescue. For many years I wanted to write this book and couldn't bring myself to start. I had plenty of things to say about writing, but I didn't feel I had any *one* thing that was important enough. Then Student X handed in the paper that appears on page 2. It, and my reactions to it, opened my eyes. I saw that many people are afraid to write—and that teachers of writing like me have made them afraid.

This idea had been tiptoeing around the edges of my consciousness before I read Student X's paper. It was a half-truth I knew without really taking it in. The paper made me take it in, gave the idea flesh and blood. I felt the feelings behind X's words: insecurity, disappointment, stubbornness, courage, joy. I understood how much it matters to an insecure writer—like X or you or me, reader—to know that writing we put our best self into will be appreciated for what we have to say (which is what matters, after all) and not dismissed because of problems we have expressing ourselves.

So much for autobiography. The point I want to make is this. Until I read X's paper, all I had to say about what counts most in writing was banal generality. X's paper gave me the peg, the specific insight and experience to which I am attaching the rest of this book.

This suggests something I have already implied: when you have a subject to write on, you needn't be interested in the whole thing. All you need to do is find some part of it that interests you, and explore that interest.

A B.A. for B.S.

Reader, are you a college student? If so, what I've just been saying applies to you with special force. In my experience college students are the most reckless generalizers. Given their head (as they should be) and a five-page assignment, a third or more will turn in papers with titles like "Social Control in America," "Electronic Media," "The Black Experience," "Taxation and Production," "The Third Dimension in Renaissance Painting," "Growing Up: A Cross-Cultural Study." Such topics are wildly too big for the scope

of the assignment. Why do students choose them? Some, with
the idealism of youth, are greatly interested in great themes.
Some, with the opportunism of youth, know that generalizing
—b.s., as it's affectionately called—is a lot easier than working with particular facts. And some, perhaps the largest
group, really have the impression that this is the sort of writing they are supposed to do. So much of what they have
learned in high school and college has come from textbooks,
encyclopedias, and think pieces in *Time, Reader's Digest, Playboy,* and the TV news that they believe they should try to
sound like these media.

No. Textbooks, encyclopedias, and think pieces use a kind
of generalized descriptive writing—overview writing, we
could call it—that requires a broad knowledge of a subject.
This is precisely what students don't have and therefore must
borrow. Such writing also requires a broad indifference to a
subject's complexities. This is precisely what most teachers
want their students to overcome. So while copying, paraphrasing, or rewriting a textbook or encyclopedia or magazine essay may work in high school, it won't in a respectable
college course.

Donald Stadtner teaches Asian art history at the University
of Texas. He tells me that when he assigns a paper he has to
take steps to avoid getting back multiple rehashes of what the
encyclopedias say. He hands out a sheet of "Rules and Suggestions for Papers" (*"Common faults:* Overdependence on
written sources; simply paraphrasing what others have said.
Lack of a clear theme. General woolliness of thought") and
forbids students to write research papers without his permission. He tells them to "depend primarily on your own obser-
vations and analyses, not on what you may find in books,"
and to analyze and interpret a specific "motif, a vessel type, a
theme or problem in jades, lacquer, ceramics, etc.; or start
with a single piece and bring in others for context and comparison."

Later, when we discuss ways of organizing a paper, we will
talk about particularization and generalization again. What
I'll say then is that competent writing needs both, and needs

incessant commerce between them. But because generalizations are so obvious, so easy to concoct, so immediately clichéd, what makes a paper new and worthwhile is almost always its particulars. Thus you should try to have your writing grow, as Stadtner recommends, from specifics: a fact, artifact, incident, person that catches your attention.

"But what if nothing does?" you say. "What if nothing interests me, and I have to write something anyhow?"

That's when it's tough. That's the problem for most writers most of the time.

"Well, it's my problem right now," you say.

Nobody said writing was easy.

"Thanks a lot."

Listen, it's not my fault you can't find anything to write about.

"You don't understand," you say. "I *have* a topic. It's assigned. I have to write on it. But I don't have anything to say."

Tell your teacher that. Ask if you can write about something else. Suggest a topic you like.

"I tried that. She said no."

Why?

"She said she gave me a good topic."

Um. She thinks she's doing you a favor—as well as herself. She knows you've got a nice complicated thing to write about, and she knows the sort of stuff you should say.

"She's keeping it a big secret."

How about the other students? Maybe they've got some ideas.

"I talked with some of them. They don't know what to write either. At least that's what they say."

There's an idea that's fashionable you might want to try. It's sort of individual brainstorming. You just *write* down as fast as you can all your thoughts on a subject, paying no attention to how you write, grammar, spelling, anything. Then, later, you read over what you've written and pick out the best things. Then you sit down again and you write about *them* in the same way.

"Free writing," you say. "Our teacher told us about it."

Did you try it?

"I kept coming up with the same garbage all the time. That's the problem—I don't have anything interesting to say about the topic. What good is it to write pages and pages of the same lousy ideas?"

Well, the hope is your ideas get better. Personally I think it's a mistake assigning specific topics. Let the students dig them up. It's the most important part of writing.

"Give us enough rope."

Exactly. But many teachers think assigned topics, even narrow ones, are good practice. They exercise the imagination— that sort of thing. Because if you're resourceful you should be able to make something of any topic. Flaubert said, *You're not interested in something? That's because you haven't paid enough attention.*

"Ouch."

He also said, *Anything is interesting when you go at it with perseverance.*

"But he was a genius."

Yes, I agree: it's hardly fair.

Seven Survival Ploys

Okay, reader. Here are seven survival ploys for when all else fails. I don't guarantee any will work for you, but I've been desperate enough, one time or another, to try them all. Some are brave to the point of folly. Some are unscrupulous. The first applies only to students; the last, to those in bureaucracies.

If you are given a topic to write on and can find nothing worthwhile to say . . .

1. Say nothing. The songwriter Tom Lehrer once said, "I wish people who have trouble communicating would just shut up." Do it. Turn in a note to your teacher: "I regret I

have nothing to say on the assigned topic." Gertrude Stein used this ploy on a final exam at Harvard. Rather than answer the question, she wrote on her paper, "I am sorry but really I do not feel a bit like an examination paper in philosophy today," and got up and left the building. It was a fine spring day. Her teacher, the pragmatist William James, gave her an A.

If you don't think your teacher yet recognizes the seeds of genius in you, or if he or she hasn't James' affection for odd behavior, do this: with your note turn in a paper on another topic related to the subject matter of the course.

2. Ignore the topic and write an explanation of why it is trivial. Speculate on why it was assigned, what you are meant to say, and how others might write on it. What others? If possible, people who would usefully comment on the topic. If you can't come up with such worthies, choose for color: as, Caesar, Karl Marx, Emily Dickinson, Bob Hope. Like ploy 1, this is a kamikaze ploy: you're almost certain to go down in flames.

3. Ignore the content of the topic and study how people involved with it talk about it and one another (English teachers call this studying the topic's "rhetoric"). Say for example you have to write on the pros and cons of capital punishment, the Equal Rights Amendment, the philosophical doctrine of hedonism, the Arab-Israeli conflict, Prince Hal versus Hotspur. Pay no attention to the issues involved. Instead, look at what opposing parties say about their adversaries. Speculate on what their language tells about them.

4. Turn the topic on its head. If you are asked to prove that something's white, show the ways in which it's black. There are conspicuous writers who have made their careers doing no more than this: inverting the common opinion. Sometimes it's the only sensible thing to do.

Student X was in my class the second semester of his freshman year. His first semester he had had to write a paper on why a college education is necessary to success. Here are the first two paragraphs of the paper:

A COLLEGE EDUCATION IS ESSENTIAL
IN GAINING SUCCESS

A college education is very helpful in gaining worldly success. There are not too many people who can come out of high school and be well prepared to face the highly complex world of today. It is the stage between high school graduation and one's first permanent job that vital changes take place in shaping an individual. When one chooses the option of college after high school there are many things he or she will learn from experience which will help them in achieving worldly success, besides the knowledge one gains in seeking a specific degree.

Of course the main reason most people go to college is to get a degree of some kind, so in turn they will obtain a well paying job. Jobs that are going to gain one worldly success demand a good college degree, therefore making it essential. For example, my roommate wishes to be a doctor and the only way for him to obtain this goal is through four years of training in undergraduate school and then on to medical school for another four to seven years of schooling (if accepted). Anyone would agree that most doctors gain worldly success for they are in demand all over the world. These doctors must be well knowledgeable in their profession, for what person would want an inexperienced doctor giving them prescriptions or diagnosing their illness. It is plain to see that a good college education is the basis in the search for success.

That is miserable. And reading it we feel what a misery it was to its writer. "Help! let me out," he is saying. "Let me stop." But Student X was dutiful. He had an assignment. He staggered on. Having shown that doctors need a college education to become doctors and thus make lots of money, he went on to demonstrate that lawyers need a college education to make lots of money as lawyers.

Now, we could improve the sentences in the paper, make them say better what they are trying to say. The paper would still be crummy. It is a paper of faint heart. It has nothing to say but what's obvious, and it says that *slowly,* again and again. (When you have something obvious to say, say it fast, once. Move on to what's worth saying.)

Student X lies down before the topic, takes it Oh-So-Seriously, as though it were profound and not a stale piece of cheese. To keep his self-respect he should have let his paper express his feelings about the topic—or better, just reversed it and made it his.

A college education necessary in gaining success? Says who? Millionaire actors, athletes, rock stars, entrepreneurs who never had one? Women college graduates whose income averages less than that of male high school graduates? Plumbers and electricians who earn more than ministers, teachers, and (would you believe) many lawyers? Besides, what is this "success"? Who said it was spelled m-o-n-e-y? Maybe college teaches you there are more important rewards, so that graduates who aren't great worldly successes are the real successes.

Simply put, Student X had to either redefine the topic for himself or locate some surprising facts to complicate our understanding of it. Where could he have gone for help in doing both things? Ploy 5.

5. Go to the library. Strange to say, some people feel that using the library is a cop-out, a confession of imaginative poverty. These people (I regret I am one) are victims of the Romantic myth that creators create entirely from within. It's not true, except in rarefied art, and that's not what we're talking about here. The writing we mean to do is pointed toward the world and our fellows in it. Hence, we have to work with what the world knows, which is to say we have to spend time slogging in the library.

This said, I do think that the library can be dangerous if you are inexperienced and don't yet have a clue what to write on. All those cards in the catalogue—and each a book! All that *knowledge* in other people's heads. You may get so intimidated you despair of writing anything yourself. (I know a topflight magazine writer who, while working on an article, can read nothing because she gets paralyzed with envy that others have *finished* their projects while she is going through hell with hers.) Or, rather than intimidate you, the sight of all that learning may make you giddy, so much so that, like the tenderfoot who jumps on an unbroken mustang, you find you're riding off in four directions at once.

But when you have a topic, there is no place like the library to change your thinking about it or give you the facts to change your reader's. Since you're looking for help, you should go to the Reference Room (or Desk). Tell the Reference Librarian what you're working on and looking for. The librarian can tell you the headings under which you will find books on your topic in the subject index of the card catalogue. If what you need is a quick variety of perspectives on your topic, the librarian may point you to the Reference Department's collection of "quotation" books, compendiums of statements, opinions, aphorisms, anecdotes—the sort of philosophical grease the newsmagazines use to make their essays slide back and forth on a subject.

If you need more substantial help—the latest facts and interpretations on your topic—the librarian will guide you through the host of indexes, abstracts, and computerized data banks that outline the contents of current magazines, important newspapers, government reports, and scholarly and professional journals. Two of the printed indexes, *The Social Science Citation Index* and *The Arts and Humanities Citation Index,* and all those on computer, allow keyword cross-referencing of the material covered. Using this, Student X could have quickly located all recent sociology articles correlating "education" and "income" or all philosophy articles discussing both "wealth" and "happiness." *The Magazine Index,* a service that began in 1977, covers 372 journals of general interest (more than twice as many as *Readers' Guide to Periodical Literature),* follows the Library of Congress' subject headings, cites reviews (of commercial products and "books, movies, drama, TV shows, records, restaurants, circus, ice capades, etc.") by name or title of the thing reviewed, and is completely updated and reissued (on 16mm "microform") every month.

Thus, when push comes to shove and you have nothing to say about a topic, go to the library, find an article that is on your subject or almost on it and that is too new or too obscure for your readers to have seen, cite the article (". . . as blank-blank says in a recent issue of *Administrative Manage-*

ment, Backpacker, Congressional Digest, Dance Magazine, Electronics, Forbes, Gourmet . . ."), and deal with an article on the topic rather than with the topic itself.

6. Look for local examples to put the topic in human terms. This is what newspeople do when they cover a big story—a pope's visit or a plane crash. They talk to witnesses and survivors ("My husband and I were having breakfast when we heard a funny yodeling sound. We looked out the window, and the garage was gone"). This is what local reporters do when there is a national story with local implications. Washington announces a recession, and the Podunk *Herald* interviews machinist Joe Doe, who's just lost his job at a downtown factory that has suffered a 27 percent reduction in orders (" 'I'm not worried now,' Doe said. 'In a couple of months I bet I won't be saying that' "). Your topic may permit you to use the same kind of local evidence.

It may force you to. There is lots of information you can't get from a library, that boneyard of the past and of "notables." The library won't tell you much about ordinary people in your town today. To get such information you have to behave like an anthropologist and do fieldwork among the natives, your neighbors. If your topic involves American voting behavior, you could interview a Republican and a Democratic precinct captain or voters (or nonvoters) from a conspicuous subgroup—the Spanish-speaking, the old, car salesmen, touch football players in the park—or simply people at random. If you are to write on mass transit or school prayer or peaceful coexistence or Johnny Carson or indeed anything the man-in-the-street has opinions about, you might try riding a city bus and asking the man-in-the-street-on-the-bus. To write about student mores, you could do worse than head for a student hangout and drink a few beers. For matters involving health, middle age, and self-renewal, consider infiltrating a figure salon. You get the idea.

If the people you interview are a representative sample, tell us so, and how. If they aren't, tell us that (we won't mind and we will like your candor). Though your method is that of the anthropologist or sociologist, you certainly don't have to

write "social science." You don't have to quantify your results, though you may if you want to and you may want to if
you have interviewed a fair number of people. Must you
interview a fair number of people? No. How many people
should you interview? As many as you want. Psychologists
say the human brain easily assimilates up to seven variables—
hence, the days of the week, the Seven Dwarfs, the seven
deadly sins. Beyond seven, things or people become a crowd,
too many to remember quickly, and we begin to need quanti-
fication. But you don't have to interview seven people. You
can interview just one, if that one says enough.

And that one can be you. You want a local informant, you
are a local—talk to yourself. There is no reason why introspective ethnography, shrewdly done, can't be as revealing as
other kinds. You may have been told to leave yourself out of
your writing because the reader isn't interested in you or
your opinions. Not true. To be sure, there is an important
kind of writing that is impersonal, done on behalf of, or to
influence, an organization or authority of some sort. We will
look at this kind of writing later when we speak of tone. But
most of the writing most of us do is personal or partly so. Or
at least, if we are bold, it *can* be. We can write from our own
perspective most of the time. We can squeeze bits of ourself,
our history, into our writing, as I am doing in this book.

And we should, because most of our readers, like most of
us, are interested in the experiences and beliefs of other people—people like you, reader. Living as and where you've
lived, you have things to tell us no one else knows in the way
you do. We want to hear them, not so much for what they tell
about you, but for what they tell about life and our society
and *us*. I am going to quote Keats again: "Nothing ever becomes real till it is experienced—even a proverb is no proverb till your life has illustrated it." Seen correctly, you are an
illustrative person, a representative man or woman. Show us
how.

Don't hesitate to write about what you know from personal experience. There is no stronger information. I have
found many insecure writers start writing better as soon as

they learn they can write about themselves without the sky falling.

7. Give up. Don't try to say anything worthwhile. Repeat what you have gotten away with before. Monthly Reports Are Required from Unit Directors above Assistant Sub-manager Rank, and you all complain you have nothing to say. Hogwash. You're just annoyed that you have to write the report and that you're going to write what you're going to write. But you're darn well going to write it—you want to keep your job. You're going to write what you wrote a month, three months, two years before, somehow reworded.

You know the case to be made in favor of writing what you wrote before. (1) It protects your ass. (2) It's true to the facts. (3) It shows the consistency of your unit's labors. (4) It gives you time for really important work. (5) Nobody reads the reports. (6) It's not plagiarizing because you're copying your-self. It might be called *recycling information*. (7) Everybody does it. Industry runs on repetition. Where would Holly-wood be without formulas to repeat?

Fine reasons. By all means reuse what you've written be-fore, so long as you do it with this sort of cynicism.

Of course there are some months when you can write the report you want to write, isolating from the evidence a theme that covers most of it and then using the theme to frame the evidence. But you can't do this when the evidence is too disparate (though that also can be a theme), lest in your at-tempt to be orderly you play the evidence false. And you can't do it when the evidence is too *un*disparate, month after month the same thing. In such a case there is no responsible way to avoid repeating (of course this can be the theme of one or more reports).

To summarize this chapter, then—

Ah, notice how that wakes you up. A summary is an excel-lent way to revive readers' interest, make them shift their weight about in the chair. A summary means something's coming to an end. Readers know they have to pay attention fast or they will miss the chance of learning whatever it was.

Besides, they feel a summary—some bold simplification that makes things stand still, as in a flash photograph—is only right after a chapter as long as this. If nothing else, as a reward for getting through it.

Remember the summary, a useful device.

As for *our* summary, how's this?

Say something that needs to be said in the context in which you are writing.

Be original in either the point you make or the evidence you use to make it. Better: be original in both. (If you can't be original in either, choose another topic.)

Look for worthwhile things to write about in what you read, of course—but also in the world around you. Especially the people.

Remember that your experience is a suitable subject for your writing. Remember also that the first time something happens to you is like the first time it ever happened.

One of the Seven Survival Ploys may buoy you up, when at sea.

3
MAKING YOUR POINT

That was one way to end that chapter. But it could have ended otherwise. It could have started otherwise. It could have taken any number of different paths in covering the ground it chose to cover. It took the path it did, and started and ended as it did, because to do so seemed to me effective in putting across what I wanted to say. The path from the start of the chapter to the end felt smooth and easy to follow, without bone-shaking bounces, mazy detours, hairpin turns.

So much for Chapter 2, which was about finding something worthwhile to write. This is Chapter 3. It is about organizing what you write.

This chapter doesn't have to start this way either. It could start, and thus be organized, quite differently. I am starting it this way because doing so demonstrates my main point about organization: there is nothing absolute about it.

There is no ideal organization. There is no perfect way to structure an argument or a paper or a chapter or a book, any more than there is a perfect way to arrange underwear in a drawer or bring up a child. I know students who, having chosen a subject and gathered quantities of information, can't begin to write because they haven't found the "right" organization. These are sensible people, who know how muddled life is, yet when it comes to writing they are still believers in the Perfect Way. They suppose that what they write can be organized to have the inevitability of an equation, $8 + 5 = 13$ or $M = Wv^2/2g$.

It can't be. Writing doesn't work that way. Writing of the kind we are talking about here deals with a world quite different from the world of mathematics or the abstract sciences. It deals with the actual, untidy world, where there are few obviously right answers or conclusive proofs and where even the simplest facts—as that this table is brown and it is better to be alive than dead—can be untrue in specific cases, certain lights, for some observers. In such a world, most truths are provisional, made for a specific occasion, and wait to be dismantled or demonstrated again—preferably in a new way. In this world it is absurd to expect anyone's writing to establish an "ultimate," $8 + 5 = 13$ truth about anything. The best we can do is create a provisional truth or two and hope to turn away before it is demolished. All we can reasonably ask of the organization of our writing, therefore, is that it clearly set forth our argument and not outrage common sense.

Actually, that's asking a good deal.

There is no Right way to organize your writing on a subject. There are many right ways. Does this mean you can organize your writing any way you please?

Yes, of course. My central message remains the same: your writing is yours—make yourself happy with it. Organize it however you think best.

The Basics of Organization

Next to choice of subject, organization is the most important part of writing. Like choice of subject, organization doesn't exist in the abstract. It exists only in the context of a specific piece of writing on a specific topic. This makes it hard to generalize about. The contemporary muckraker Jessica

Mitford has a sensible essay on writing in her collection of magazine articles, *Poison Penmanship*. She spends five hundred words on organization, which she calls "all-important; here is where the article does or does not come together." Her conclusion: "I can offer no useful guidelines here, as each piece of work will present its own unique problems. One can only hope the solution will occur in a sudden blinding flash of insight."

I am still waiting to be blinded by a flash of insight, but I agree with Mitford that all organizational solutions are ad hoc, custom made to meet a specific problem. I agree with her, too, that each of us has to solve our own problems of organization, just as we had to solve the problem of what to write. Nonetheless, I am eager to put forward a few ideas— provisional truths—for you to consider as you go about your organizing.

To start with, let's define what we are talking about. What is the organization of writing? I say it's the order in which a piece of writing discusses the various aspects of its subject. What comes first, what is next, what after that, what comes last. In deciding the order in which aspects of a subject are discussed, the organizer may also decide what gets left out of the discussion, since leaving something out is often an organizational choice (one decides, for example, that something is too peripheral to be discussed in the space given).

Since organization determines the order of what you write, it must be done before you start writing. The question is, how much before?

Edward Thompson, editor-in-chief of *Reader's Digest* magazine, has written one of the International Paper Company's ongoing series of advertisements, "Power of the Printed Word," which aim to help "all of us to *read* better, *write* better, and *communicate* better." Thompson takes the view we learned in grade school: we must have a paper fully organized before we write a word of it. He says: "You can't write clearly until, *before you start*, you know where you will stop." He tells us to make a complete outline of what we are going to say.

This is the advice most composition teachers give—though some, like Donald Murray, prefer to call the outline a "design" and permit the design to be mental rather than written down. Before a writer writes, says Murray, he "must have, in his mind's eye or on paper, an idea of where he is going to begin and where he is going to stop."[1]

Having an outline or a design ahead of time is one of those things that's a great help to people it's a great help to. Robert Caro wrote an outline for his monumental, much praised, Pulitzer Prize winning, 1,246-page biography, *The Power Broker: Robert Moses and the Fall of New York City.* Ina Caro, Bob's wife, who helped him research the book, has told me, and Bob has cautiously confirmed, that the outline was at least as long and maybe a good deal longer than the final text. The outline gave the content of each paragraph in such detail that Bob was able to actually write some of the book as fast as he could move a pencil.

That is a splendid way to write something: have it all thought out ahead of time and then simply put it down on the page. I wish I could do it. I can't, though, and have stopped trying. I can make an outline beforehand, but I don't follow it because while I'm writing better connections and better ideas occur to me. It strikes me as natural that they would since it is when I write, not when I outline, that I work most closely with my subject, see its complexities most fully, and can best estimate what readers will have trouble understanding.

To be sure, I organize my writing beforehand as much as I can. I know, for example, most of what I will say in this chapter: I made a list of points to cover before I began writing. But I made no outline. When I started writing I didn't know what order I would treat the points in. Though I have covered some of the points, I still don't know the order I will use with the points remaining. At this moment there are three or four different paths I could take. I will decide which

---

[1] Donald M. Murray, *Writer Teaches Writing,* Boston, 1968, p. 7. [I'm changing over to numbered footnotes here, reader, because I want you to see both numbered and asterisked footnotes in use. Footnoting is discussed in Chapter 5.]

one to take as soon as I can. As far ahead as possible. But perhaps not until the start of the paragraph in which I make my move. If this happens, I will still be organizing my writing before I do it—but only *just*.

Here's my point. There are people who can outline their writing far in advance. Good for them. There are people who can't. Worst luck, I am one of them. For people like me organizing isn't only done in advance, it is done continuously. Until the final word of a piece is written it is being done.

Continuous Organization

I have chosen the path I will take for the next few pages. (How many pages I don't know. As many as it takes me to explore the topic I'm now going to raise.)

I just said organization can be done continuously. What does this mean? It means that writing can be well—that is, logically—organized moment by moment as a writer goes along, even though the writer doesn't know where he or she will be a page hence, to say nothing of where he or she is finally going to get to. You notice that this is what I have just done. Two paragraphs back I suggested that people who can't outline their writing beforehand have to organize it continuously. In this paragraph I am explaining what I meant. Thus what I say now grows out of what I most recently said. There is an obvious link between them. The path from one point to the other is smooth. By continuous organization I have made a reasonable transition.

Of course there were other reasonable transitions I could have made. As I said, there were three or four paths I considered taking. I took the one I did because it answered what seemed to me the most pressing question: how to organize your writing if you don't outline it.

I am sure many writers use the technique of continuous organization, though I haven't seen a discussion of it and had to give it a name. I believe writers would use it better if they understood that it is a legitimate technique and followed it scrupulously. It is a technique of somewhat alarming spontaneity, requiring many leaps in the dark—an *existential* technique, the writer Norman Mailer would say (he, surely a continuous organizer). There is nothing absolute about it: writers move their attention one way or another because it feels right at the moment.

Nonetheless, the technique has its own rules and limits. The writer makes leaps in the dark, yes, but always from a firm footing. In high school did you have to try the flying rings? You were supposed to run forward hanging onto the first ring, then jump and swing and catch the second ring, letting go the first, then swing and catch the third, letting go the second, and so on, hand over hand across the gym.

Writing by continuous organization is like that. To make a good transition all that you need to do is make a smooth grab of the next ring. You will then go flying forward through the air, but so long as you find another ring to grab onto, you will not stall or fall. You will go swinging boldly on, losing and gaining momentum, to all appearances as though you know where you are going. Which may not be the case. You may be discovering your trip as you make it, recognizing your destination only when you get there.

This suggests the main difference between continuous organization and the flying rings: in writing your destination isn't necessarily known ahead of time; there is no set path across the gym. At most points of transition there are several rings to choose from, not just one, and they may lead off in irreconcilable directions. A direction chosen may prove a dead end. You may land yourself in a corner and be unable to move on to another subject. In such a case there may be nothing for it but to backtrack to the place the bad choice was made, tear up the intervening paragraphs, and choose another direction. Norman Mailer has said he is reluctant to write novels because a wrong choice made at one point can mean months of subsequent writing have to be thrown out.

The thing that is similar about the flying rings and continuous organization, the thing that makes them worth comparing, is the emphasis both put on adjacency. In the flying rings you only move onward if you catch the next ring. If the ring you try to catch isn't near enough, you land on the floor. The same in writing: there must be an obvious connection between what you just said and what you are now saying, or your writing falls to pieces.

The best way to make sure there is a connection between what you just said and what you are now saying is to make the connection explicit. This is easy. You do it by repeating at the start of a paragraph a word or words that occurred in the preceding paragraph, usually near the end. (Note how the first sentence in this paragraph repeats words from the last sentence of the last.) Continuous organization is built on the establishment and use of keywords. Such words are the rings on which you swing from paragraph to paragraph and topic to topic.

Once you get skilled in making explicit connections, you will sometimes find you can postpone repeating a keyword until deep into a new paragraph, you can substitute a synonym for it that has additional meanings and gives you a new keyword to play with, or you can leave it unspoken, implicit. You will find that apparently opposing words, like *but, however, conversely, nevertheless,* and *on the other hand,* actually connect things by turning them round and examining their backsides. You will find, too, that connection can be made where connection is denied, as when a writer says, "I am now going to talk about something else."

I would now like to talk about something else, but I'm not going to yet because I have one thing more to say about continuous organization. (Remember this moment, please, reader. I will refer to it later.) The goal of continuous organization is the goal of every scheme for organizing writing: to present a subject clearly to the reader. The assumption behind continuous organization is that if each moment in a piece of writing is clear the piece of writing as a whole will be clear. There are those who deny this assumption. They say that every piece of writing needs an overall logical form or structure, like a medieval cathedral. Such people are absolutists, and I have rejected their assumption, and explained why, in the first pages of this chapter.

In fact, however, continuous organization *does* give writing a logical form and structure. The form is that of a straight line running from one point to another to another to another:

Just because the point of conclusion isn't known in advance doesn't mean a journey isn't logical.

Absolutists distrust the straight line. They find it too open-ended—as it is. The logical form they prefer is the one St. Thomas learned from Aristotle: the circle. They want every piece of writing, every argument, to begin and end at the same point:

In textbooks on writing they have set down as the organizational ideal the structure Aristotle saw in a few blood-soaked Greek plays: introduction of a subject, exploration of the subject, conclusion. The popularizers among them say that a piece of writing must say what it will say (the introduction), then say it (the body), then say it said it (the conclusion). Thus is the circle closed: Q.E.D., the assertion validated.

Circular Organization

A circular structure is excellent for some kinds of writing. Lawyers like it because it focuses evidence on a central point, the conclusion announced at the beginning ("Ladies and gentlemen of the jury, I am going to prove that my client could not possibly have . . ."). I make a circle whenever I have one thing I want to demonstrate or refute ("There are three reasons why I deserve a raise. First . . ."). If a circular structure accommodates what you want to say, by all means use it.

If my experience is any guide, though, you will find that the writing you care most about seldom lends itself to circular organization. Too much ground has to be covered, too many disparate points joined together, and only a line can do the job. That is why, whether organized ahead of time or at the last minute, most writing uses the flying-ring method.

Personally I am glad of this. Such writing seems to me more exciting. Its landscape keeps changing, offering surprise. Because you as reader don't know where the path will lead, you have the fun of exploration and discovery. Reading becomes more an open-ended experience. Your relation to the writer is continually in question. You can't know ahead of time whether the writer will be able to coax you up the next hill, across those slippery stones, through that dark wood. At any juncture you may cry out, "That's cheating. No fair," and close the book. Such a possibility helps keep both reader and writer on their toes.

The weakness of continuous organization—its open-ended indeterminacy—is usually a strength, or so I believe. Conversely, the strength of the circular method—its predictability —I often find a weakness. Because the circular method announces its conclusion at the start ("I am going to prove that . . ."), the conclusion itself, when it comes, is redundant, a letdown. You know how it sounds:

Thus I have amply demonstrated that . . .

TV has indeed influenced our generation, its personality, its values, its humor, even the clothes it wears.

An analysis of the evidence supports the view, then, that the Whig Party, having moved too little for the Abolitionists and too much for the Southerners, lost constituents on both ends of the political spectrum and in consequence ceased to be a party capable of electing a president.

It seems to me I heard that song before.

I am going to take advantage of my continuous organization and end this section of the chapter with an unlooked-for paragraph of advice on how to avoid or minimize redundancy when you use circular organization. Circular organization demands that your conclusion repeat your introduction —demands, that is, that the circle be closed. Well, close the circle, but don't only do that. Certainly don't rub it in like this:

○

Instead, close it lightly or come so close to closing it that everyone sees you *could* close it. Then for a sentence or two or a paragraph or, if you have written a book, a couple of pages, bring in another theme or idea, even if only slightly related to your subject, and finish your writing on a tangent, thus

𝟞

or thus

𝟞

This technique, a version of what journalists call the "kicker" at the end of the article, lets a little air into your writing, opens up your subject to the world, and helps suggest why people actually ought to be interested in what you have said.

Below I "open up" two of the redundant endings I quoted above:

Since TV has influenced today's college students so much—our values, our humor, even the clothes we wear—why don't we think better of it? Why do we laugh at the daydreams it tries to stuff in our heads? Somewhere along the line we have learned values we respect more than those retailed on television. Our parents won't believe it, but we are going to turn out to be human beings.

An analysis of the evidence supports the view, then, that the Whig Party, having moved too little for the Abolitionists and too much for the Southerners, lost constituents on both ends of the political spectrum and in consequence ceased to be a party capable of electing a president. The politics of compromise can be bad politics.[2]

---

[2] I was dissatisfied with how little I had to say about circular organization and so made an appeal to an old friend, Daniel Kripke, M.D., psychiatrist, sleep researcher, and professor in the medical school at the University of California, San Diego. I remembered that Dan, while a freshman at Harvard, got a C on a paper he had written for a French class. He wasn't accustomed to getting C's and so very reason-

Undoing Introductions

Thus you end a piece of writing, I suggest, by pointing your readers back to the big world, freeing them from the little world you made.

But how do you *start* a piece of writing?

Simple. You tell what your subject is and get to the first point you want to make about it as quick as you can.

And what point should you make first?

It doesn't matter. I said on page 7 that I generally put first the point I want most to make. (You notice I did that in this chapter, my first point being that it is a waste of time trying for perfect organization because no such thing exists.) But you may decide your paper or article or chapter or book will move more coherently if you begin with another, less important point. Fine. Try it.

What matters is that you announce your topic and get to *some* point fast. One of the most useless ideas your teachers have drummed into you is that of making introductions to

---

ably looked his teacher up and asked what was wrong. The teacher, a Frenchman, told him that the paper was perhaps all right in America but wouldn't do in France. "You haven't followed our system of organization," he said. Dan asked what the system was, and the teacher told him. As Dan remembers, the system was to divide a paper into three parts: introduction, main body, and conclusion. Each of these had three parts:

    I. Introduction
        A. Why the topic is interesting
        B. What's going to be discussed
        C. A hint at the conclusions
    II. Main Body
        A. Thesis
        B. Antithesis (whatever contradicts the thesis)
        C. Synthesis
    III. Conclusion
        A. Summary
        B. Major concluding ideas
        C. Is it a topic for the future? Where do we go from here?

Dan followed this system thereafter in French courses, and occasionally others, and never got less than an A.

everything you write. Here is Jim Corder's *Handbook of Current English* explaining how to start a paper:

A STATEMENT OF PURPOSE OR POINT OF VIEW. This should not be a mechanical statement ("In this paper I am going to give you my reasons for majoring in political science") or a flat rewording of the assignment, but a natural lead into the topic:

When I decided to enter the university, like most freshmen I had only the vaguest notion of what subject I intended to major in. But now after two quarters of haphazardly chosen course work, and after a good deal of self-analysis, I have decided that there are at least four good reasons why I should major in political science.

Bushwa. The revision ("When I decided to enter the university," etc.) is the work of a goody-goody trying to snow the teacher. It has lost the strength of the original: "In this paper I am going to give you my reasons for majoring in political science." That's beautiful. That's telling the truth. Readers are so amazed when a writer tells the truth they are likely to keep reading just to see if it happens again.

The notion that every paper needs an introduction encourages drivel like the following:

THE INFLUENCE OF MOVIES ON COLLEGE STUDENTS

America's college generation has been influenced by many things this year. The current political events, top recording groups, and a new experience of beginning college mature a young adult in certain ways. However, the forms of entertainment subconsciously effect one more than other influences in today's world. One such form is film.

There was no reason to wade through all that. We could have had the topic in a sentence ("This year's movies have several messages for college students like me") and the first point in another ("The first is: Grab for all the gusto you can, but keep a hand on your wallet").

The problem with introductions is that writers, particularly bad writers, use them to clear their throats. I asked the freshmen in Student X's class to write about the influence on them of a book, movie, TV show, play, or record of their choice.

One student's first paragraph is given above. Here is another student's first paragraph:

Changes have been an obvious factor in most modern cultures. There have always been changes, but it seems that the younger generation thrives on changes. If a young person of today is not entertained in some way, then boredom strikes, causing him to demand changes in his life style. Some people say that the need for instant entertainment is caused by the lack of imagination in the young people of today. To elaborate further on this subject, many qualified authorities feel that this gradual decrease in imagination has something to do with the unbelievable importance of television in our culture.

With the truisms, exaggerations, and wafflings cut out, that paragraph reduces to its last sentence, which can be more sharply put, as for instance: "Many people, some of them authorities of one sort or another, believe that television blunts the imagination of those who watch it." A stronger sentence, but the student still hasn't gotten to her subject: the influence of a particular TV show on her.

Don't clear your throat: get to the point. If you are going to discuss TV's influence or the gold standard or union membership among white-collar workers or post-Bauhaus architecture or the 1980 U.S. presidential election, don't start off, "Changes have been an obvious factor in most modern cultures." If you are discussing conflict of loyalty in Sophocles' *Antigone,* don't begin by telling us that not much is known of Sophocles' life or that Aeschylus wrote the first Greek tragedy or that tragedies are sad plays filled with conflicts or that most sisters love their brothers. Information of this kind is *unnecessary foreground* to the subject you are going to treat. Cut the foreground: get to the subject where it starts to be interesting. (What do I mean "interesting"? I tried to suggest what interesting writing is in Chapters 1 and 2, but here are five words I could have used just now in place of "interesting": useful, unexplored, surprising, complex, controversial.)

Many novice writers are devotees of what my friend Bob Crunden calls the "genetic fallacy." They think that before discussing a subject they must give its antecedents—the remoter the better. Thus a paper on professional football begins,

In about 250 B.C. there was the first wrestling match in the Roman Coliseum. Later, knights played games on the Crusades. British schoolboys participated formally in sports.

And smoke went up the chimney and Santa Claus came down, but they got us no closer to the subject.

You are going to begin writing what you mean to be writing *sometime.* Why not right away?

The Strategy of Nonfiction

Okay. You begin by announcing your subject. Then you make your first point. Then . . . ?

Then you "prove" the point. I put the word prove in quotation marks because if you are writing on an original, complex, useful topic you won't be able to *prove* anything. Not conclusively. Not with the open-and-shut definiteness that $8+5=13$. You will be able to *suggest,* but not prove. Some philosophers argue that nothing can really be proved, since mankind doesn't know things as they are, only as they appear to us. By this view even scientific truths based on the carefullest measurement of supersubtle machines are necessarily tentative. Gregory Bateson explains: "As a method of perception—and that is all science can claim to be—science, like all other methods of perception, is limited in its ability to collecting the outward and visible signs of whatever may be the truth. Science *probes;* it does not prove."[3]

So you don't *prove,* you "prove." Having asserted something you present evidence or examples that corroborate or demonstrate or validate your assertion. You make a point and then substantiate it. This is what I am trying to do all the time here. In the last paragraph I claimed that science doesn't dis-

[3] *Mind and Nature,* New York, 1979, p. 30. [You notice that no author's name is given before the book title. This is because the author is named in the text to which the footnote refers.]

cover the truth about things, and then cited words by the anthropologist-philosopher Gregory Bateson to support my claim. Did Bateson's words prove I was right? Of course not. We don't know that I'm right about this or anything of consequence I'm telling you. Bateson's words merely supported what I had said.

Without planning to we have come to the bottom of the subject we are studying, which is the craft of expository writing. We see the simple way such writing works: points are made and then substantiated. We hear the beat of a great two-stroke heart:

> assertion . . . demonstration
> thesis . . . example
> opinion . . . justification
> claim . . . evidence
> generalization . . . particulars
> argument . . . "proof."

All writing that means to convince a reader by rational means moves to this beat. All such writing is an interchange of assertion and demonstration, thesis and proof.

Many writers don't realize this. They *assert* well enough—indeed get downright preachy—but they don't "prove" their cases. This is one of my most frequent criticisms. The following are from three final comments I wrote on students' papers:

You have only one thing to say and say it in every paragraph. (It is *"Dispatches* is a terrific, powerful musical made from a powerful book."") But you never PROVE this; you never show WHY the musical (or the book) is terrific or powerful. You assert, but don't demonstrate.

Your autobiographical material, which begins well, is too soon abandoned for preaching. It is easy to preach, though of course hard to preach *well* (as it is hard to do anything well). One hungers for more than opinion, though—which is of course what preaching is. One hungers for *evidence.*

I agree with your opinions but don't feel I've learned much from your statement of them. What you give us is a sort of editorial or sermon (both of which genres are okay); its sentiments do you credit and make good sense (to me at least). But I don't see that you've found any way of "proving" and demonstrating the truth of your argument, nor of stating it memorably or vividly. The paper seems "true," then, but it doesn't break new ground and thus doesn't seem to me really useful.

Winning an Argument

The question is of course, *how* do you demonstrate an assertion, justify an opinion, "prove" a case?

This question troubled me when I was starting to write my Ph.D. thesis. I knew the question had been long debated, back to the days of Plato and the Sophists. But I was naïve enough to think it could be answered. Since my thesis was going to put forward a few fairly original suggestions, I wanted to know the method I should use to persuade readers the suggestions were correct. Fortunately I came across a book that stopped my worrying about method.

The book, E. D. Hirsch, Jr.'s *Validity in Interpretation,* told me what I have told you: most issues of consequence can't be definitely proved. Because "meaning is a matter of consciousness," Hirsch said, "it could never be shown that two different persons entertained identical meanings" about anything. As a result, he explained,

in order to avoid giving the false impression that there is anything permanent about an interpretative validation [which is to say, a "proof"] or the consensus [of belief] it aims to achieve, I now prefer the term "validation" to the more definitive-sounding word "verification." To verify is to show that a conclusion is true; to validate is to show that a conclusion is probably true on the basis of what is known.

This is not to say that a correct interpretation is impossible. "Correctness is . . . the goal of interpretation and may in fact be achieved, even though it can never be known to be achieved." Correct interpretations are achieved through what Hirsch called "probability judgments" and "informed guesses" ("probability judgments are informed guesses"). But how are such good guesses made? Hirsch's answer set me free by saying that I already knew:

In the course of making any of these probability judgments, the interpreter's chief concern is to narrow the class [of unknowns he is dealing with]; that is to say, his chief concern is to find out as much as he can about his text and all matters relating to it. That everyone has always known this conclusion is another illustration of the fact that the logic of uncertainty is the logic of common sense.[4]

The logic of uncertainty is the logic of common sense. I read that sentence over, then read on a little more not taking in the words, then came back to the sentence and stared at it. It was just what I wanted, the license I had been looking for. It told me what to do when I was unsure how to make a case. It said, "Make it the best you can. What is reasonable to you will be reasonable to other people, if anything you say is going to be. We all behave the same when we are lost."

The way you make a case (says common sense) is by bringing forward evidence that supports your point of view. That is all you can do to persuade others to your side.

What about evidence that runs counter to your view? You bring it forward also. Not to do so is bad sportsmanship—and violates common sense as well. After all, nobody who knows anything about your subject is going to trust you and your opinions if you overlook evidence harmful to your cause. If, on the other hand, you yourself introduce such evidence, examine it, explain why it doesn't weigh as much as other evidence you cite, maybe your readers will agree with you, obviously a fair-minded person. In any event your discussion of the competing evidence gives depth and controversy to your writing and should help you hold your readers' interest.

The evidence you present, whether or not it is self-contradictory, aims to give your argument depth: the depth of detail, particularization, complexity. As I said earlier (see page 43), in most writing it is the detail that matters most, the

4 New Haven, 1967, pp. 37, 33, 170–71, 173, 175, 198. [Author's name and book title are both given in the text.]

main argument being a generalization people know in one form or another. In making your case, you naturally use the strongest details you have, which always means the most convincing examples, and often the most colorful and intricate ones as well.

An example. By the summer of 1973 Department of Justice attorneys in Maryland had a mass of sworn testimony linking Spiro Agnew to extortion, bribery, and conspiracy involving road contractors while he was Baltimore County Executive, Governor of Maryland, and Vice-President of the United States. The attorneys didn't get to bring Agnew to trial on these charges, which were dropped when the Vice-President, in a plea bargain, agreed to resign his office and plead no contest—the equivalent of guilty—to income tax evasion. As part of the bargain, though, the attorneys had the right to present to the court hearing Agnew's case an "exposition of the evidence" they had against him. This exposition took forty pages. It was written to make sure the American public understood that Agnew deserved the disgrace he suffered.

The exposition is a compendium of devastating evidence, of Agnew soliciting and accepting bribes: cash in plain brown envelopes, some of which were delivered to him in the Vice-President's chambers on Capitol Hill. The detail is abundant, repetitive, and finally boring. No doubt realizing this, the attorneys put the richest detail at the end of the exposition, hoping it would be noticed and quoted—as indeed it was. Lester Matz, an engineer who swore he had paid Agnew $37,500 over the years in exchange for road contracts, was pressed by a close associate to make a legitimate contribution to the 1972 Nixon-Agnew campaign. The attorneys told the rest of the story in two sentences:

Matz declined. When the close associate continued to press him, Matz complained about these solicitations to Mr. Agnew, who told Matz to say he gave at the office.

This detail, the only thing I remembered from the exposition until I read it again, does its job of damning Agnew so well because it is unexpectedly funny, shows Agnew's clever side, and shows, no less, his huge indifference to his own wrongdoing.[5]

How Much Is Enough?

Granted you choose the best evidence you have to make your case, how much evidence do you use?

As much as is appropriate to the length you are writing at.

Length is a problem for novice writers. You remember the assignment I gave Student X's freshman composition class: to write a paper beginning "The chief problem I have with my writing is . . ." Here is Student Z's paper:

MY WRITING

The chief problem I have with my writing is finding a way to make my papers longer. I am usually a woman of few words, and some teachers believe that that is one of my faults. When I try to lengthen a paper, the meaning is sometimes lost or dilluted, and the paper becomes awkward. As you can see, this paper is very short. What am I to do, Mr. Stott, write my papers short and sweet or long and awkward?

To which I made this response:

Short and sweet, by all means. Nevertheless, this paper would be improved by an instance, an example or two of how (for instance) you weakened the meaning of an earlier paper by expanding the paper's length. I'm sure you understand why we'd like such an example: it would demonstrate what you say and thus convince us. Without an example it is hard to blame anyone but you for having "lost" the meaning of something you wrote.

But you touch on an important point, and I like your boldness.

Student Z touched on an important point. Teachers tell you not to write more than you have to say, and yet they assign you papers of fixed length: five, ten, twenty pages.

[5] The full "Exposition of Evidence" is in the New York *Times*, October 11, 1973, pp. 36–38.

How do they know you will need to take that long? How do they reconcile their advice with their assignments?

Easy. When they assign a twenty-page (or five-thousand-word) paper, they are not merely telling you to write twenty pages. By implication they are also telling you to define your subject in such a way that its complexities take twenty pages to describe and analyze. Thus, if you haven't twenty pages of worthwhile stuff to say on a subject, you have flubbed the assignment.

Writing assignments of fixed length are intellectually defensible, I would argue, but I don't think novice writers should be given them all the time. Novice writers need to learn for themselves how much they must say to cover a subject adequately. This is learned by trial and error, and they need the opportunity to go wrong. For many of them it is a liberation to discover that a subject can be treated at different lengths, indeed *any* length. "Any idea, any book can . . . be suggested in a sentence or expounded in twenty volumes," said the sociologist C. Wright Mills, who went on to reduce his 412-page book, *The Power Elite,* to this: "Who, after all, runs America? No one runs it altogether, but in so far as any group does, the power elite."[6]

Whether a subject is appropriately treated long or short, and *how* long and how short, depends on its importance and, even more, on the context in which you are writing. It is true, as an old saying has it, that brevity is good both when we are understood and when we are not. It is also true that virtually everything we read is too long. Nonetheless, Student Z's paper was too short for the context in which it was written— our freshman English class—and for the purposefulness it needed to have in consequence of that context.

Student Z touched on an important point, but because she

[6] *The Sociological Imagination,* New York and London, 1959, p. 31. Can the book you are holding in your hands, WRITE TO THE POINT, be summed up in a sentence or two? Of course: "What you write is generally much more important than how you write it. So if you have something worthwhile to say, write each sentence clearly, follow commonsense organization, and obey a few arbitrary rules of grammar, your writing will be adequate to most purposes." That's not all the book says, but it's the main point.

did nothing to substantiate and "prove" it, it didn't *seem* important to her. Because she spoke so briefly, she didn't appear to have much to say.

And this is of course the usual reason novice writers can't write long papers: they don't have enough to say. For them the problem of length isn't a problem of organization. Rather it is the crucial problem we began the book with: the problem of what to write.

I spent our first two chapters on this problem. You will be pleased to know I won't say another word about it.

A Basic Rule

I won't say a word about it because, for better or worse, I have *done* that topic. I gave it my best effort, and to discuss it again now would violate the important rule of organization I want to close this chapter with.

This rule the writer Dwight Macdonald calls "the great basic principle of organization: *put everything on the same subject in the same place.*" Discuss a topic once, as thoroughly as you want, and don't bring it up for discussion again.[7] Macdonald, who wrote for *Fortune* magazine in his youth, remembers that,

when an editor casually explained this trick of the trade to me . . . my first reaction was "obviously," my second "but why didn't it ever occur to me?", and my third that it was one of those profound banalities "everybody knows"—after they've been told.[8]

Once told, we see immediately why this all-of-a-topic-in-one-place rule makes sense. We want to organize our writing

[7] Earlier in this chapter, on page 59, I told you I wanted to talk about something other than the topic at hand but wasn't going to do so. I continued discussing the topic at hand because, as I explained, I had a further point to make about it. If I was going to make that point anytime in this book, I had to make it then. I wouldn't be able to discuss the topic later for the same reason I cannot now discuss what to write on.

[8] Review of W. A. Swanberg, *Luce and His Empire,* in Macdonald, *Discriminations: Essays and Afterthoughts, 1938–1974,* New York, 1974, p. 269.

so that it will be as easy as possible to follow. Thus we want it
to take one of two logical forms: a straight line

or a circle

When a writer doubles back to discuss again something discussed earlier, the straight line becomes an overhand knot

and the circle a drunken web

Logic and simplicity are lost. Readers are too.

The chapter ends here, though there is no reason it has to.
It was organized by the flying-ring method, whose logic is
that of a line going from point to point to point

A line being open-ended, the chapter could go on forever.
But it stops at the end of this paragraph. I have made the
points I wanted to make and other useful points that occurred
to me while writing. I started with a list of things to say about
organization. I haven't covered every item on the list, but the
few that remain now look trivial to me compared with what
has gone before. It often happens with continuous organization that some of the ideas you start with get left out in the
actual writing, can't be stuck back in anywhere later, and
aren't important enough to tack onto the end. Best to ignore
them and to stop. Abruptly, if you don't want the bother of
finding a better way.

4
GETTING IT DOWN

All right. You have something worthwhile to say (Chapters 1 and 2) and know how to organize the saying of it (Chapter 3). This chapter will tell you how to put it into words.

To this point our book has had a plot. Now the plot thins. This chapter and Chapter 5 are divided into separate topics introduced by subheads. Some topics take many pages; some take one. The chapter is like a series of poker games between us, reader. You will try to guess what I am going to say under a given subhead, and I will try to cheat your expectation, surprise you with the New and Useful (remember Chapter 2). If I can't do this, I'll move the discussion to another topic by saying things extraneous to the original topic but connected to it in my argument (continuous organization: remember Chapter 3). There is nothing unusual about such a competitive strategy: writers and readers, like teachers and students, can't help working toward different ends.

This chapter is built on an assumption about writing. The assumption:

Writing is good when its meaning is put as simply as it can be.

Most writers take a while making their sentences as simple as possible. Thus, if this chapter had to content itself with making just one recommendation (as it conspicuously does not), that recommendation would be:

Take your time writing. Revise what you first put down. Readers don't know how long you take getting a sentence right (a sentence is right when its meaning is put as plainly as it can be), but they know when you get a sentence wrong. And when you do, they know that either you are an incompetent writer or you don't care much about what you are saying. Those alternatives you may not want to accept.

Blank-Page Paralysis

Before they get a word on paper, many writers clutch. "They have so internalized criticism of their writing that paralysis sets in," says Nancy Packer, head of Stanford University's freshman English program. They stare at the empty page—the first of many they have to fill. They sharpen pencils, chew the top of a pen, tap on the typewriter's space bar. Every word and phrase they consider writing their self-censor shoots down first.

You may know the feeling. I do. I don't leave the page blank. I write a few words. But immediately I see they are wrong and cross them out. I used to spend a couple of days suffering, and quitting and unquitting, before I came up with a first paragraph I could build from. This still happens some of the time.

What I try to do now, though, as I've told you (page 7), is to start off by writing, in a sentence or two, what I want most to say. It often takes me several hours to put this into words as well as I can, but when I do I usually find I have had to say other things, both before and after.

So here are two suggestions for lessening blank-page paralysis:

1. Write down some words, *any* words. Then cross them out.
2. Write down, in a sentence or two, what you want most to say. Justify it.

A third suggestion. Do you remember we joked about "free writing" (page 44)? We joked about it as a way of finding fresh things to say.[1] But it is a good way of fighting blank-page paralysis. Like many composition teachers, Nancy Packer recommends that students with writer's block "free write": "write nonstop, continuously, never lifting the hand from the paper, putting down whatever thoughts occur, and when no thoughts come, filling in with repetition or nonsense." Packer says, "This method helps to break down that instant self-censorship which grips many very good students when they start to write."

Diction

Let's say you have broken the ice jam. Your words now pour forth on the page. What words? What words do you write with?

Here is my short answer: the simplest possible words.

Below is my long answer.

Diction II

Your diction is the words you use in speaking and writing, your vocabulary. If you are like most people, you think your vocabulary deficient. Most of Student X's classmates said this was the main problem with their writing. One wrote: "I feel that my vocabulary is not enriched enough to write a good college paper." Another: "I always strive for better words to express myself, rather than rely on the same hackneyed syllables." A third:

I am not confident in myself enough to just write down my own thoughts in fear of sounding naive and unintelligent. So, in contrast, I try to substitute longer, more intellectual words than my

[1] I have had second thoughts on this matter. See Appendix B, page 211.

thoughts are capable of. In the end, my paper sounds intelligently written—but ridiculously composed.

It isn't only students who think their diction needs beefing up with longer words. Self-help books promising "powerful" and "effective" vocabularies are consistent good sellers. One such book, advertised in national magazines, uses as its come-on a line something like "Know Why Your Boss Has His Job and You Don't?" The answer given—that the boss has a bigger vocabulary—apparently strikes some people as plausible.

As that ad suggests, vocabulary-building books trade on our fear of inadequacy. It is just this sort of fear I want to fight because, as I have said, I want you to feel better about your writing, not intimidated. This particular fear is a dandy one to fight because it is both widespread and pointless.

When you are talking, you don't need a bigger vocabulary to say what you want to say. You just need to say it. The same when you write: you just need to say what you want to say. You may find a word escapes you for a time and have to rummage in a dictionary or thesaurus to find it—or forget about it, sleep on it, and let it come to you. But the simplest word that says what you want to say—as for example *simple* instead of *uncomplicated*—is the best word to say it.

You must have heard this before. I'm sure people have told you to write with short simple words. They may have told you what Winston Churchill (1874–1965) said about diction: "Short words are best, and the old words, when short, are best of all." That's generally true. Most of us would write better with smaller vocabularies, just as we would read better if we read slower, moving our lips.

We have been told to use simple words, but we don't do it. Why? Fear is part of the reason. Simple words don't seem impressive enough. Last summer I accompanied the American critic R. W. B. Lewis while he interviewed the British writer V. S. Pritchett. I knew that Pritchett had taught for several years at American colleges, and at the end of the interview I asked him what he thought of American students' writing. He cleared his throat and said he thought it "professorial."

"Professorial?" I said, myself a professor.

"Yes," he said, "a number of the students wrote sentences I didn't understand—full of long words like a professor's. I'd say to them, 'What do you mean by this?' pointing to a sentence. They'd say, 'Why, that means . . .' and they'd tell me using their own words. And I'd say, 'Why didn't you *say* that, in those words?' And they'd say, 'You mean I'm allowed to?'"

Pritchett laughed. I laughed. Neither of us felt very good about laughing.

What Pritchett said is a strong criticism of the job we teachers are doing. We may think we are telling our students to use simple words, but our students are getting a different message from us and from the culture. The message is: Protect yourself. Use safe, official-sounding words. Write like someone who is too important to write simply.

Behind the message, prompting it, is fear of a particular kind. Most Americans, like many people in the modern world, don't have social rank assigned us on the basis of birth, inherited wealth, sex, religion, ethnicity, party membership, or place of education. In a real way we are what we make ourselves, and we depend on our jobs, our professional roles, to establish our status. Because our place in society is self-made, we tend to be insecure about it and to look for ways of asserting it. One of these ways is through language. As the TV performer Dick Cavett has observed, "These days an airplane pilot doesn't tell us he expects a bumpy ride; he anticipates experiencing considerable turbulence. A policeman doesn't say the suspect got out of the car; he relates that the alleged perpetrator exited the vehicle." The pilot and policeman use big words to assert their professional roles and consequent social worth.

Since pilots, policemen, and professors sometimes suffer status anxiety, it is understandable that students and beginning writers do, who have yet to achieve much status. For such people an inflated vocabulary is a sign of fear, yes—but of aspiration too. In Ayn Rand's novel *The Fountainhead*, the reporters on a newspaper strike against its publisher, Gail Wynand, who, to keep the paper running, sends out copy boys to get the news.

Most of the stuff they sent in was of such quality that Wynand was forced past despair into howls of laughter: he had never read such highbrow English; he could see the pride of the ambitious youth who was a journalist at last.

Rand's book is full of romantic balderdash but here she is exactly right. It is insecure writers who use big words.

What do I mean "big words"? Look at what young writers write:

Thoreau believes the implementation of the principle can sometimes necessitate an abdication of and withdrawal from society at large.

Their speeches [Martin Luther King, Jr.'s and Malcolm X's] are testaments of their fundamental disparities, exemplifying not only political differences, but also rhetorical dissimilarities.

The neighbors cease to be merely co-workers at a monotonous job in the factory and are rendered interesting people with a value that is no longer negated by material circumstance.

Look at the kind of words we chuckle at, as here in columnist Russell Baker's "translation of Little Red Riding Hood into the modern American language":

Once upon a point in time, a small person named Little Red Riding Hood initiated plans for the preparation, delivery and transportation of foodstuffs to her grandmother, a senior citizen residing at a place of residence in a forest of indeterminate dimension.

In the process of implementing this program, her incursion into the forest was in mid-transportation process when it attained interface with an alleged perpetrator. This individual, a wolf, made inquiry as to the whereabouts of Little Red Riding Hood's goal as well as inferring that he was desirous of ascertaining the contents of Little Red Riding Hood's foodstuffs basket.

Or look at the diction of a jargoneer, like this expert on friendship:

Lack of intensity of relation is a dependable biproduct of the failure or reduction of peer-group reinforcement in cases of cognitive controversy in the sources analyzed (except, apparently, sports) and more than that leads to the institutionalization of repetition-behavior in cases where the relational contact was not terminated on the first occasion.

You know this kind of talk. It is sludge language—vague, depersonalized, pompous, clichéd. It is the gobbledygook of bad social science, slobbering professionalism, and good old b.s.

There are many ways to avoid it. One way is never to use jargon—that is, any word belonging to a profession but not in common use. A second way is to avoid words longer than two syllables (as much as you can). A third way V. S. Pritchett suggested: translate what you write into the words you would use to express the thought in conversation. A fourth way R. W. B. Lewis pointed out to me a generation ago when I was his student. It made a difference to me, and I want to tell you it, though it takes another paragraph.

Lewis read a paper of mine and told me its diction was ponderous. I think he may have used the word "clunky." He asked whether I had read the poet John Crowe Ransom's essay "On Shakespeare's Language." I said no—at least I hope I said no because I hadn't read it. Lewis told me what the essay said and sent me off to read it. Ransom's essay, most recently reprinted in his *Poems and Essays* (New York, 1962), argues that Shakespeare found a way to balance the two kinds of words we have in English: Anglo-Saxon words—like *sweat* —and Latinate words—like *perspiration.* Ransom says that when Shakespeare has Macbeth look at his hand, bloody from Duncan's murder, and say

> Will all great Neptune's ocean wash this blood
> Clean from my hand? No, this my hand will rather
> The multitudinous seas incarnadine,
> Making the green one red,

the reason the stupendous "Latinical explosion" in the third
line works is that the lines surrounding it are plain, nearly
monosyllabic, Anglo-Saxon "native English." Ransom:

The last line is specially primitive, having three strong accented
words juxtaposed with some peril to the clear syntax; for we wonder, I think, whether to take *one* as going with *green* or with *red;* but
a locution like *solid red* while explicit would be mildly Latinical, and
it is apparently Shakespeare's idea to follow up the Latinical third
line by about half a line of primitive language even with its natural
disabilities.

What Lewis wanted me to understand from the Ransom
essay was that I should write mainly with words derived from
Anglo-Saxon English—Old English, as it is called. When
there are several ways to say something, I should choose the
"primitive" one and write, for example, "Ransom *made up*
the adjective" rather than *concocted* or *fabricated* it. He wanted
me to understand Shakespeare's trick of countering big
words—like the *—able, —ance, —ate, —ity, —ive, —ment,* and
—tion words imported from French and Latin—with old simple words, thus making the big words lighter. I used this trick
a page back when I mixed big and little words, foreign-born
and native, in the list ". . . bad social science, slobbering
professionalism, and good old b.s."

It is true that some writers and linguists claim there is no
difference between the Anglo-Saxon and Latinate words in
English, or indeed that the latter are preferable. Richard Mc-
Millan, a British writer and teacher of writing, has argued
that rather than use "he said" and "she said" to set off dialogue, a writer should "enliven the narration" with descriptive synonyms:

"He smiled," "she consented," "he ingeminated," "she interpo-
lated"—these are examples of what I mean. I can give nearly 300
examples of such synonyms for "said" (far more than in Roget's),
and in my task as a tutor in short story writing, I drill this point
home to my pupils. (I am somewhat qualified, having won the first
prize in the best African short story in *Drums* magazine, out of
10,000 entries.)

But surely, Mr. McMillan, there's a difference between *he said* and *he ingeminated*. One sentence says something. The other calls attention to its cleverness in saying something, rather as you call attention to your cleverness.

The linguist Mario Pei has written, "Avoid Latin derivatives; use brief, terse Anglo-Saxon monosyllables"—and then pulled the rug out by announcing that his statement contained only one non-Latin word: *Anglo-Saxon*. That too is clever, but it doesn't invalidate Lewis' point that one should write mainly with Anglo-Saxon words. Sometimes a Latinate word is the shortest way to say something, as I think *invalidate* was in the last sentence. Furthermore, as Pei demonstrates, there are Latinate words so brief (from Middle French *brief, bref,* which comes from Latin *brevis)* and terse (from Latin *tersus,* meaning "clean" or "neat") they seem Anglo-Saxon. But these words (*face* is another) are the exceptions. In general, the Latin-derived words in English have several syllables. Often there are shorter Anglo-Saxon-derived words that mean the same thing. And even when the Anglo-Saxon word isn't a monosyllable—as *slobbering* is not—it has a different feel, a different quality from most Latinate words (*feel* is Anglo-Saxon, *quality* is Latin). That is the point.

Consider the words Winston Churchill used to rally his countrymen and the English-speaking peoples in the dark days of the Battle of Britain. The best-remembered words sound like this:

I have nothing to offer but blood, toil, tears, and sweat.

Never in the field of human conflict was so much owed by so many to so few.

We shall not flag or fail. We shall fight in France, we shall fight on the seas and oceans, we shall fight with growing confidence and growing strength in the air, we shall defend our island, whatever the cost may be; we shall fight on the beaches, we shall fight on the landing grounds, we shall fight in the fields and in the streets, we shall fight in the hills; we shall never surrender.

The words Churchill used are overwhelmingly Anglo-Saxon, the old short words he thought best of all. Consider the "we shall fight" paragraph written during the British evacuation from Dunkirk. When Churchill uses a Latinate word—*confidence,* say—he immediately balances it with a primitive monosyllable, *strength,* having tied them together not only with an *and* but with the same Anglo-Saxon adjective, *growing.* He speaks of Britain not as a "nation" or "country," both words French borrowings, but as an *island* (from *īgland,* an Old English cognate with Old Frisian *eiland* and Old Norse *eyland*—all derived from a prehistoric Germanic word). He sees the British people fighting (the Anglo-Saxon root is *feohtan)* on the beaches, in the fields, and in the hills—all plausible native terms for native locales. They are to fight also on the *landing grounds,* two Anglo-Saxon words used despite the fact their reference is ambiguous. Does Churchill mean "enemy disembarkation zones"? Perhaps—but he would never use such Latinate words because they hold up the white flag of bureaucratese. Or does he mean "airports": we will fight them on the airports? This too is possible. Presumably he avoids the word "airport" because it makes the war seem trivial; "airport," a continental word (French *aéroport,* Italian *aeroporto,* Portuguese *aeroporto,* Spanish *aeropuerto),* doesn't have the resonance of "landing grounds." As Churchill describes it, the battle for Britain will proceed from the beaches and landing grounds through the fields to the urban agglomerations, but of course he can't use these words either. He won't even speak of cities (from the Latin *civis, civitatis).* The fight has to be in the streets (Anglo-Saxon *strēt, strǣt)* and then, when it is abandoned there, back in the unsubmitting hills. After such drumfire of repetition and Anglo-Saxonisms, Churchill lets up the pressure in the last sentence's last word. He allows himself to say *surrender,* a word from the French *(se rendre,* to turn oneself in), who were just then on the point of surrendering, and not a nice word.

Churchill used Anglo-Saxon words because, to English speakers, they are stronger than Latin words. They cut deeper into us. They are bone words, while the Latin words

only reach our brains. From Latin we get "courage," beautiful word. From Anglo-Saxon we get "guts," an ugly ferocious
word of much more force. Old English is, as Ransom said, a
primitive language, as primitive as father and mother, wife
and child, husband and friend, birth, death, kindness, truth,
hope, hearth, home—all Anglo-Saxon words. (For comparison, the French equivalent of the last three "h" words is
espoir, foyer, and *domicile.*) Old English is the language that
names what matters most to most of us. Reason enough to
write in it as much as possible.

But here is a surprising fact: writers of English haven't
always felt this. Look at a piece of published writing from the
eighteenth or nineteenth century. Odds are it is written with
a much higher percentage of Latinate words than published
writing today. Here, at random, is Walter Scott, from his
novel *Woodstock:*

The inferior personages of the grand jail-delivery at Woodstock
Lodge easily found themselves temporary accommodations in the
town among old acquaintance; but no one ventured to entertain the
old knight, understood to be so much under the displeasure of the
ruling powers; and even the innkeeper of the George, who had
been one of his tenants, scarce dared to admit him to the common
privileges of a traveller, who has food and lodging for his money.
Everard attended him unrequested, unpermitted, but also unforbid-
den. The heart of the old man had been turned once more towards
him when he learned how he had behaved at the memorable ren-
contre at the King's Oak, and saw that he was an object of the
enmity, rather than the favour, of Cromwell. But there was another
secret feeling which tended to reconcile him to his nephew—the
consciousness that Everard shared with him the deep anxiety which
he experienced on account of his daughter, who had not yet re-
turned from her doubtful and perilous expedition.

Here, also at random, is Edgar Allan Poe, "The Premature
Burial":

For several years I had been subject to attacks of the singular disor-
der which physicians have agreed to term catalepsy, in default of a
more definite title. Although both the immediate and the predis-
posing causes, and even the actual diagnosis, of this disease are still

mysterious, its obvious and apparent character is sufficiently well understood. Its variations seem to be chiefly of degree. Sometimes the patient lies, for a day only or even for a shorter period, in a species of exaggerated lethargy. He is senseless and externally motionless; but the pulsation of the heart is still faintly perceptible; some traces of warmth remain; a slight color lingers within the centre of the cheek; and, upon application of a mirror to the lips, we can detect a torpid, unequal, and vacillating action of the lungs. Then again the duration of the trance is for weeks—even for months; while the closest scrutiny, and the most rigorous medical tests, fail to establish any material distinction between the state of the sufferer and what we conceive of absolute death.

I'm not saying Scott and Poe aren't good in their way. I am saying their way is no longer ours.

Scott and Poe, like all storytellers, are weaving spells. They do this in large measure through their diction and the tone it creates. Different though they were in personality, and different though their writings are in theme and purpose, their diction is similarly Latinate and their tone is similarly gloomy and serious. This tone, which critics have come to call "high seriousness," is standard in nineteenth-century literature in English. Poe wrote in it because he believed it "the most ethereal—in other words, the most elevating and most pure" —and thus the most likely to realize "the Human Aspiration for Supernal Beauty." Like Poe, Scott used the tone knowing it to be elevated. Unlike Poe, he joked at its pretentiousness. He said his readers didn't care what he said so long as he kept the tone, which he called the Big Bow Wow.

Nineteenth-century readers loved the Big Bow Wow for a good reason: they were taught to. Educated readers, and hence most writers, were classically trained. The language they studied closely wasn't English but Latin, sometimes supplemented with Greek. Their ears were attuned to lengthier words, nobler tones, than we are now. People wrote English with Latin in their heads and tried to duplicate its sound.

Latin lost its hold on American education in the early decades of this century and on British education after World War II. As a consequence, the music of good written English changed. A starker sound gained favor. The bits of Churchill's speeches I have quoted are conspicuous examples of this Anglo-Saxon sound, and it is significant that Churchill, untypical of schoolboys of his class and time, didn't learn Latin or Greek. He was considered too stupid (his word) to write anything but the "most disregarded thing . . . mere English." He spent three years parsing sentences in a remedial class. Churchill:

Thus I got into my bones the essential structure of the ordinary British sentence—which is a noble thing. And when in after years my school-fellows who had won prizes and distinction for writing such beautiful Latin poetry and pithy Greek epigrams had to come down again to common English, to earn their living or make their way, I did not feel myself at any disadvantage. Naturally I am biassed in favour of boys learning English. I would make them all learn English; and then I would let the clever ones learn Latin as an honour, and Greek as a treat. But the only thing I would whip them for is not knowing English. I would whip them hard for that.

Ignore his bullying, reader. He is proud because he didn't turn out a dumbbell after all. He was a ninety-seven-pound weakling and look at him now, ready to whip the rest of us for not writing English.

But we *can* write English. Vocabulary is no problem. Anything we can think of saying we have the words to say; at worst, we have the words to explain what we can't say. Of course we have to keep learning the new words the world drops upon us, and words useful in school or at work. But the vast majority of the words we need for writing we learned at our parents' knees by age ten. We only need what Churchill so magnificently possessed: the guts to use them.

A final point. When a word is right, it's right. If you need to use it again, don't beat the bushes for a substitute: use it again. Here's what not to do: "I always strive for better words to express myself, rather than rely on the same hackneyed syllables."

The word is *word*. Don't be fancy—repeat it all you need

to. It's just the sort of word people pay attention to: a plain, one-syllable, Anglo-Saxon word.

But You Disagree, Reader

You say you have been told to use exactly the sort of words I tell you not to use: long, pretentious, academic words.

Hmm. I wish I could tell you such advice is wrong. It's *generally* wrong, I'm sure of that, but it isn't always wrong. The world is a complicated place. There are times when you will benefit from using an inflated vocabulary.

You will quickly discover when those times are. If you are a student and your teacher tells you to use big words, that's a time. If you are a junior executive writing stuff for your boss' signature and your boss has a penchant for Latinate circumlocution, that's a time; toss a few ornaments into your prose. If you are a lawyer writing for lawyers, or indeed any specialist writing for fellow practitioners, you may have to use the going jargon, though it makes you unintelligible to the uninitiated.

You decide what diction to use, then, as much by whom you are writing for as by what you want to say. You choose words that fit the tone you think will best convey your subject to your readers.

Tone

The tone of a piece of writing is the attitude the writing has toward its subject and its audience. The tone of Milton's *Paradise Lost* is elevated, ominous, and sad. The tone of E. E. Cummings' poetry is cheerful and sometimes flippant to the point of nihilism. The tone of this book is . . . well, what do you think, reader? What adjective describes it best?

As we just observed, the tone you write in is determined by what you want to say and whom you are writing for—in short, by the writing's *context*. Sometimes the context is so relaxed and personal that you can write just as you please. You're writing for yourself in a diary or journal and no matter how you say something you'll know what you mean. Or you're writing for friends and relations who know you well enough to see through how you say something to what you mean to say.

At other times the context is so formal and impersonal that you have little choice but to write that way too. You are writing for people whom you don't know, or don't know well, and you are writing for them *because of their, or your, professional role.* You address these people not as individuals but as links in the great chain of bureaucracy and status accumulation: as secretaries and presidents, creditors and bad loans, complainers and complaint departments. You talk to them in Official Prose, the language they speak to you, the language of impersonality.

For example, you are writing a business firm:

Dear Sir or Madam:
Jane Doe, who is applying for a management trainee position with your company, has asked me to write a letter of recommendation on her behalf. I am pleased to do this, because I know Ms. Doe well and have great respect for her intelligence, diligence, resourcefulness, good humor, ambition and promise.
I have known Ms. Doe since . . .

Or you are writing a government grant agency:

Research activities to be undertaken during the funding period to meet the objectives specified in the original proposal are summarized in Table I, Appendix A. Project activities are divided into three areas to make optimum use of the restricted time period, to avoid duplication of efforts, and to take advantage of particular specializations and skills of the part-time researchers employed. The three major areas are (A) Historical-Archival Research, (B) Field Research, and (C) Quantitative-Demographic Research.

Or you are writing *on behalf of* an organization of some sort, any sort. And you keep the minutes:

The meeting was called to order at 10:25 by the president. The following members were absent: Brown, Johnson, Jones, Smith, and Williams.

The first order of business was the reading of the minutes of the last meeting. The minutes were read and approved.

The second order of business . . .

Or you write a polite no:

Dear Ms. Doe:

This letter is to thank you for your application for the position we had open in our Marketing Division and to inform you that we have decided to give the job to another applicant.

As you are aware, competition for employment in our industry over the last years has been intense, with the qualifications of prospective employees steadily rising. We find it necessary, therefore, to reject a large number of highly qualified candidates.

We regret this and wish you well in your search for suitable employment.

Are you annoyed at the impersonality of Official Prose? I used to be too. Then I decided I was wrong: such writing has to be pretty much that way. Of course you can write clearly, even if your tone is impersonal and your diction bureaucratic. You can even stage a mild rebellion and put a little humor or a few personal asides in official writing you sign your name to. I often do this, though I suspect it is generally a waste of time. I spent years in officialdom reading memos for and from government agencies. The writing was standard muck, with occasional pages that tried to be well written or entertaining or "individual." I was usually grateful for such pages, though I got annoyed when the writer had tried too hard. But here's the point: I didn't give the information on those pages more consideration than I gave information made in duller prose. I was a bureaucrat; I followed the rules of the game.

Bureaucrats have guidelines. A case meets the guidelines or it doesn't. The presentation of the case isn't supposed to cut any ice and, I believe, seldom does. Dean Acheson said that while he was Secretary of State he got eloquent memos from a subordinate who counseled him to do things he, Acheson, disagreed with. He found the memos difficult to refute until he had another subordinate translate them into bureaucratese, whereupon the weakness of their case was plain. Acheson, a good writer, was susceptible to good writing. Most bureaucrats, like people in general, are less susceptible; they are interested in content, not form.

But perhaps a mild rebellion isn't enough for you. You want to blow the impersonal tone away, thumb your nose at the bureaucratic context, write as you damn well please. And you can do it. In the letter recommending Jane Doe, for example, you could call her a hot tomato. In the organizational minutes you could write, "The next order of business was your hung-over secretary trying to find the one decent pen he owns, which had snuck from his pocket into—as it turned out, as he turned it out—the lining of his foul-smelling jacket." In your polite letter saying no you could conclude: "We find it necessary, therefore, to reject a large number of highly qualified candidates as well as a much larger number of obvious frauds and buffoons. I trust you know in which group you belong."

You could do this, but you shouldn't. Such gross violations of tone and context are bad strategy and bad taste. Whoever writes this kind of thing does it for attention. He is grandstanding. He wants readers to look away from what he is writing and at the writer, him. He wants to be noticed for the brilliant fellow he is. And noticed he is—as a conceited boob.

Context determines appropriate tone, reader. No use fighting it. A bureaucratic context requires a tone gentled with impersonality.

But there are other contexts and other tones. Not all writing is personal, on the one hand, or formal and bureaucratic, on the other. There is a wide range of writing in between.

In between is the most interesting writing, I think: serious, informal writing, like what I'm doing in this book. Such writing isn't rigid and formulaic the way Official Prose is. It has some of the freedom of personal writing and can modify its tone as it goes along from careful to boisterous, laid-back to chilly. Like Official Prose, it means to communicate with people the writer doesn't know. Unlike Official Prose, it means to reach them as people, individual human beings, not role-playing professionals.

But how? How can a writer establish rapport with a reader who is a stranger? a reader who is both one and many: a specific person sitting by a white lamp in Illinois and the "general" reader, target of every trade book and supermarket magazine? How do you speak to an abstraction—to someone you want to treat as an individual but don't, *can't,* know?

You talk the way I'm trying to talk to you, general reader. You talk as though to

- Someone reasonable
- Someone who can be persuaded with evidence and common sense
- Someone alive
- Someone who can be surprised, angered, moved to laughter and tears, but not long condescended to, confused, or bored
- Someone sophisticated enough to be interested in the world, in other people, and in what you think and why you think it
- A skeptic. A truth-teller. Someone who reads your writing and says:

Your subject doesn't interest me and I don't believe it interested you. Pointless.

Or:

What you say is a rehash of what we know. You say it poorly.

Or:

You write well enough to say anything you want to. Too bad you have so little to say here.

Or:

Interesting. I wish you had taken the time to write this more as it deserves to be written. Still, interesting.

Or:

I'm convinced. You have a case worth making and make it well. You may even be right.

When you don't know the reader you are writing for, you must consider your reader a person of good sense, humanity, and candor. Someone like you at your best. (If you write something you think dumb—a sentence, a book—there is no chance this reader will disagree.) To such a person you must talk modestly. Of course you want to impress your reader. One always wants one's reader to be impressed—bowled over, if possible. (There is a playful animosity between writers and readers, as between all artists and their audiences. You hear writers say, "I'm gonna show that bastard, knock him outa the chair." And readers: "What is this crazy bastard up to?") But you can't impress *this* reader with boasts or empty cleverness. Being just as shrewd as you, this reader sees right through such dodges. You have to have something to say and hand it over, as frankly as you can, for the reader to judge.

Because the unknown reader you write for is a digest of your virtues, you may find *actual* readers a disappointment—lazy, nitpicking, overappreciative. And when an actual reader judges your writing, you will use that judgment to judge him or her:

He let me say that? Some help he is.

Uh-oh. A grade of C. "There is nothing remarkable here." What does she want?

That's nice. "Not a happy phrase," she says. Ha ha. She's right.

"Interesting point!" That's bad: he's *surprised.* The rest of the paper must be even duller than I thought.

On the basis of their comments you will decide which of your readers to pay attention to, and when, how much, and why:

I can learn from this guy. He's too egotistical to read closely, word for word. But he asks the right questions.

I don't know about her. She won't help me with ideas much. She may get me to untangle my sentences.

He's a fool. He's *nice,* he's fun to work with. I just can't listen to him.

You will treat your reader's opinion of your writing as just that: opinion, not truth.

This is the time to say something I trust I have already implied: your reader's opinion of your writing, like your opinion of him or her, is subjective. It is *his* opinion, though if he is competent he has pointed to facts in your writing that support the opinion, thus working to objectify his subjectivity. Still, the opinion is subjective. Other readers not only *might* disagree with it, they certainly would to some extent. And none of them and not all of them together would have the final word. We have very few final words. We don't know the sort of writing God prefers—God hasn't told us. (Even if God had, would that wipe out our sense of what we like?) We assume that Samuel Beckett's *Waiting for Godot* is better than Erskine Caldwell's *God's Little Acre,* if only because Beckett is so much duller (my opinion). But we can't ultimately prove our assumption any more than we can prove ballet superior to baseball or craps. It is silly to claim that our view of something is more than our view of something.

So when I tell you to use old short words—opinion. When someone else tells you to use long words—opinion. When a teacher gives you a C on a paper—opinion. Does everybody have a right to an opinion? Certainly. Are some people's opinions better than others? Of course. Whose opinions are better? That also is a matter of opinion. Teachers have the authority to turn their opinions into grades because they have gone through an accrediting process that includes having their writing criticized by accredited teachers; thus their subjective opinions have presumably been modified by standards common to other literate writers of the language. But this doesn't mean that a given teacher's opinion is any better than anybody else's. It may be worse and, having the weight of a profession behind it, more harmful.

Where does this leave us? What tone should your writing take? Who should you write for when you are writing blind? I gave you my opinion, or implied it, several pages back. If you don't know who you are writing for, if (to say the same thing) you are writing for people in general, I suggest you write for yourself, your shrewdest self, the general reader in you. You may have heard writers say they write for themselves. I think this is what they mean. To write this book for you, reader, I am writing it for me.

Your inner reader is the only guide you have always available. It may not be a good guide: if you are a bad (form) writer, you probably have a bad inner reader. But it can be improved. That is why, while you are beginning to write seriously, you need criticism from actual readers whose opinions you respect. That is also why you are still reading this book.

Should Your Writing Refer to You as "I"?

It depends.

I would like to say flatly yes, since yes is the sensible answer. After all, you are the one doing the writing, and as the critic Roland Barthes points out, "the detours on *one, we* or impersonal sentence make no difference": readers always know an *I* has written what they read. But this is an instance where the sensible answer is too simple.

So: it depends. It depends on the context.

If you are writing on your own behalf about things you know from your experience, then of course refer to yourself as "I," as I am here. Referring to yourself otherwise—as "we" or "one" or "the writer" or "this researcher" or "your author"—is stilted and self-important. (Some critics think the use of "I" is self-important. That is exactly backward.) "I" is correct in contexts like the following. The historian Johan Huizinga apologizes for the incompleteness of his book *Homo Ludens: A Study of the Play Element in Culture:*

The reader of these pages should not look for detailed documentation of every word. . . . To fill in the gaps in my knowledge was out of the question. I had to write now or not at all. And I wanted to write.

The journalist Joan Didion tells how she gets some of her best stories:

My only advantage as a reporter is that I am so physically small, so temperamentally unobtrusive, and so neurotically inarticulate that people tend to forget that my presence runs counter to their best interests.

But as we have noted a number of times, most recently in discussing tone, not all your writing is on your own behalf. You may write for an organization or a periodical. In such impersonal or *multi*personal contexts, you are not speaking only for yourself. Thus you must refer to yourself as *we* or *our store, this office, the company's management, the editors of this newspaper,* etc. When Thomas Jefferson wrote,

We hold these truths to be self-evident, that all men are created equal, that they are endowed by their Creator with certain unalienable Rights, that among these are Life, Liberty and the pursuit of Happiness

he was writing on behalf of the committee appointed to draft what came to be called the Declaration of Independence, and of the Continental Congress that appointed that committee, and of the colonies that sent representatives to that Congress, and of all the people in what would become the United States of America who then favored independence from Great Britain. Sufficient reason to use the first person plural.

Similarly, when you write as an expert, critic, or scholar, you are writing on behalf of an assumed collection of authorities like you. Thus you may refer to yourself as *we* ("Those of us who watch the Soviet Union's behavior toward its dissidents . . .") or as *one* ("One suspects that even the divine Bach didn't realize what he had wrought").

There is yet another way to use the first person plural. Note the third word in the paragraph before last, "But as we have noted . . ." This *we* is you and me, reader: writer and audience. I could have written, "But as I have noted . . ." but I didn't want to underline the fact that this is my book and I am causing things to happen here. I wanted you to feel engaged as a participant in our endeavor, so I had you join me in recalling something mentioned earlier. This writer-and-reader "we" is a handy way to evade the exclusive "I."

A small concern.

In general, use "I" whenever the context permits and as often as you want. Readers know "I" is one word that always tells the truth.

Try Not to Sound Self-Important

It alienates readers.

A famous comedian was asked how he made himself funny and sympathetic to his audience. The comedian (was it Jack Benny?) answered, "Forget everything you've done right. Remember the boo-boos."

When writing, keep quiet about what you've done right. Humility is the best policy.

Don't You Have to Avoid Contractions and Say "Do Not" Instead of "Don't" and "You Have" Instead of "You've"?

No.

What we just said about the use of "I" applies here too. Whether or not you use contractions depends on the tone you want, which depends in turn on the context. The more impersonal the context, the more formal the tone. The more formal the tone, the fewer the contractions.

There is a pecking order among contractions. The "n't" contractions (don't, aren't, haven't, and the like) are felt to be more formal than the subject-and-verb contractions (I've, you're, she's, we'd, and so on). Hence the "n't" contractions are used in contexts where the subject-and-verb contractions are not. In this book, for instance, I am generally using "n't" contractions but not subject-and-verb contractions. Both of these contractions are more formal than the verb-and-verb contractions *(should've, could've, would've),* which I'm not using here at all.

You understand there is no correlation between the formality or informality of a piece of writing and its goodness or badness. Some of the best writing is informal: witness *The Adventures of Huckleberry Finn,* which is full of contractions and slang. Most bad writing is formal: witness the reports bureaucracies grind out, the papers college students write, their teachers' books.

How to Write Sentences

When members of the audience finally loosen up and ask the Conspicuous Writer the question nearest their heart, it comes out,

Do you compose at the typewriter?

Do you write in the morning?

Do you do a full draft before you start revising?

Does drink help?

Drugs?

Behind this question, however phrased, is the real question: *How do you do it? Writing looks easy—how come you do it successfully and I don't?*

By learning how Conspicuous Writers put words on paper (is there anything special about the paper? what color is it?), the audience hopes to plug into some of their power.

The audience knows better, of course. The audience—people like you and me, reader—knows that the way words get down on paper has nothing to do with the value of the words or what they are saying. But we know this intellectually. In a primitive way we still feel that the Conspicuous Writer must have some trick we could learn, some secret.

There is no secret. I won't convince you of this, except intellectually, and you already *know* it. I can't convince myself. I keep feeling I am going to do something different one day and begin writing stuff that will make people hold their foreheads in amazement:

But here is the truth.

- Conspicuous Writers write their sentences the way you and I do—one word after the other.

- Some Conspicuous Writers write easily, some write with difficulty.

- Some Conspicuous Writers would agree, and some would not, with what I've already said about tone and diction and with the how-to-write advice I'm going to give you during the next fifty pages.

But

- Most Conspicuous Writers would tell you that how they write something is normally of less importance than what they write.

Thus the first thing to be said about writing a sentence, however short, is the first thing we said about writing anything, however long:

- Have something to say.

Have something precise to say in each sentence before you write a word of it. Once you have written the sentence out— indeed *while* you're writing it out—you may decide that what you wanted to say when you began writing it isn't what you now want to say. Fine. Scratch that sentence and write another saying what you now want to say.

That doesn't negate the first rule of sentence writing:

- Before you write a sentence, know what you mean it to say.

The second rule of sentence writing is even more important. In fact it is so important that all the other suggestions I will make are its offspring. It is:

- Say what you mean to say as plainly as you can.

Don't "Frontload" Too Many of Your Sentences

Here is a paragraph from a student paper:

During the early years of the series, chief nurse Margaret, alias Hotlips, played by Loretta Swit, was often the target of Hawkeye's sarcasm, but later she changed substantially. Unlike her lover, weak-chinned Frank, she was always competent, a fact admitted by Hawkeye and others. While under Frank's influence she was an unthinking martinet. Having suffered Frank's departure and a brief marriage to a beefy golden-boy colonel, Margaret has grown more human, has learned to trust herself and others more. Though she remains absurdly patriotic, she has come to see herself as a person rather than as an officer's wife. Rejecting the sexual advances of her superiors, she reaches out to her nurses and to others in the camp community.

All the sentences in this paragraph are, to coin a term, front-loaded. The usual pattern of English sentences is subject-verb-predicate. (In that sentence the subject is *pattern,* the verb is *is,* and the predicate is *subject-verb-predicate.*) The sentences in the quoted paragraph postpone the pattern by inserting a phrase or clause *before* the subject. Such frontloading muddies our path through the sentence and is a nuisance when it occurs constantly. I recommend that you frontload no more than one sentence in four or five.

We said in Chapter 3 that you should get to the subject you are writing on without a meandering introduction. Get to the subject of your sentences the same way.

The Best Subject for a Sentence

Whenever possible you should make person-words—like *I, she, we, they, Hamlet, Mr. and Mrs. Smith, most blind people*—the subject of your sentences. When the subject has to be something nonhuman, modify it, as often as you can, with a person-word like *my, your, Jimmy Carter's, left-handed batters'.* Readers know where they stand when a person-word is the subject of a sentence or modifies that subject, and they may not when the person is removed. Compare the vagueness of

Expectations clouded perceptions

with the plainness of

Our expectations clouded our perceptions.

I realized how important person-words are many pages back when I noticed how often you, reader, are the subject of my sentences. I need "you" to make what I say as clear as possible. Compare the fuzziness of

In the absence of a known reader of a piece of writing, it is necessary to write for an imaginary reader who is considered to be a person of good sense, humanity, and candor

with the sharpness of

When you don't know the reader you are writing for, you must consider your reader a person of good sense, humanity, and candor.

Readers don't get tired of person-words as sentence subjects. They don't notice them. Up to this point every sentence in this section, except the two I give as bad examples, has a person-word subject. (In the command sentences—"Compare the . . . ," ". . . modify it . . ."—the person-word subject is an unspoken "you.")

Plain writing uses lots of person-words. Note, for instance, the subjects of the sentences in the "How to Write Sentences" section on page 98. The subjects are, in order:

> members of the audience
> it
> you (three times in a row)
> drink
> drugs
> question
> you
> writing
> you

I
the audience (three times)
we (twice)
secret
I
you
I (twice)
truth
Conspicuous Writers
some Conspicuous Writers (twice)
some ["Conspicuous Writers" understood] (twice)
most Conspicuous Writers
and so on.

In addition to person-words, plain writing uses lots of pointing words like *this, that, these,* and *such.* One of Jimmy Carter's accomplishments as President was getting the federal government to address the American public in clearer prose. When the Internal Revenue Service questions you about your income tax these days, it includes a slip of paper with the following paragraph on it. Note the person-words and the helpful "this" and "these."

The Paperwork Reduction Act of 1980 says we must tell you why we are collecting this information, how we will use it, and whether you have to give it to us. We ask for the information to carry out the Internal Revenue laws of the United States. We need to to ensure that taxpayers are complying with these laws and to allow us to figure and collect the right amount of tax. You are required to give us this information.[2]

---

[2] This paragraph, good though it is, would be clearer if the ". . . why we are collecting this information . . ." were further personalized to include "you," the taxpayer who must provide the information, and if the word "collecting" were made less vague. Why not: "The Paperwork Reduction Act of 1980 says we must tell you why we are asking you for this information, how we will use it, and whether you have to give it to us. We ask for the information to carry out . . ."

Avoid Sexist Language

More than half our race is female. When you are generalizing about human life, try to find words that refer to women as well as men.

Though I have tried to do this here, I have not always succeeded. I refused clumsy expedients like the following, from a collective bargaining agreement between a teachers' union and Boston University:

> The college or university teacher is a citizen, a member of a learned profession, and an officer of an educational institution. When he/she speaks or writes as a citizen, he/she should be free from institutional censorship or discipline, but his/her position in the community imposes special obligations. As a man or woman of learning and an educational officer, he/she should remember that the public may judge his/her institution by his/her utterances. Hence, he/she should at all times be accurate, should exercise appropriate restraint, should show respect for the opinions of others, and should make every effort to indicate that he/she is not an institutional spokesperson.

A reader asks how I would revise this. Rather than make the subject "the college or university teacher . . . he/she," I'd make it "college and university teachers . . . they."

Pinpoint People

My wife once wrote a paper that mentioned in passing an idea of Hegel's. Her teacher, Gordon Craig, circled the word Hegel and wrote in the margin, "Who's he?" Craig later explained that was what *his* wife did when his writing introduced people without pinpointing them.

"There are quite a lot of Germans named Hegel," he said. "You and I remember that a *famous* Hegel was a philosopher. But some readers may not. It's easy to remind them: 'Hegel the philosopher.' "

There are certain people so conspicuous they don't need to

be pinpointed: Plato, Aristotle, a score of the greatest artists, several dozen political leaders and villains, the founders of the big religions, Muhammad Ali, Elvis Presley, other current saints.

Otherwise, the first time you mention somebody, tell who they are in a word or phrase:

her teacher, Gordon Craig

Jessica Mitford, the contemporary muckraker

a psychologist like J. P. Gilford

my uncle George Merrell

John Foster Dulles, who was President Eisenhower's Secretary of State

poet Henry Wadsworth Longfellow.

Verbs, Active and Passive

A tractor squashed her new Porsche. We call this sentence "active," and say its verb *(squashed)* is in the active voice, because the sentence's subject *(A tractor)* commits the action shown in the verb.

Her new Porsche was squashed by a tractor. We call this sentence "passive," and say its verb *(was squashed)* is in the passive voice, because the sentence's subject *(Her new Porsche)* receives the action of the verb. In a passive sentence the agent that produces the action is not the subject of the sentence, as *a tractor* is not the subject here. The agent is often not mentioned: *A window was broken. The shoplifter must have been astonished to be stopped at the door.*

You have probably been told to write active sentences, make your sentence subjects perform the action in your verbs, avoid the passive voice. You have probably also been told to avoid the verb *to be* because it appears in passive sentences and is dull.

Writing teacher Richard Lanham argues that a sentence like *A goat kicked him* is much better than *He was kicked by a goat.* Lanham has a horror of the source of action being stuck in a sentence's predicate, as happens in the prepositional phrase *by a goat.* "The drill for this problem stands clear," he writes, using *stands* to avoid the insipid *is.* "Circle every form of 'to be' ('is,' 'was,' 'will be,' 'seems to be') and every prepositional phrase. Then find out who's kicking whom and start rebuilding the sentence with that action."[3] Eliminate the verb *to be.*

Or rather, replace it with a flashier verb. "Don't choose [a verb] that is dull or merely serviceable," says William Zinsser, a writer and teacher of writing. "Make action verbs activate your sentences." Zinsser gives a list of the sorts of verbs he likes: "flail, poke, dazzle, squash, beguile, pamper, swagger, wheedle, vex."[4]

Lanham's and Zinsser's advice is the standard advice English teachers give. I think it is bad advice.

I feel this strongly because I was given similar advice in high school, and it ruined my writing for a decade. My fault, of course. I was one of those earnest fools who believe teachers know what they are talking about. I thought my English teacher was right. It seemed reasonable that active verbs would be more interesting than passive ones and that peppy, unusual verbs *(burble, bumble, bleat)* would be more interesting than the verb *to be.* So throughout college and my twenties I spent a good deal of writing time larding sentences with colorful verbs like *jostle* and *scurry* and *lard* and twisting sentences to avoid *is* and *are.* The results? Overwriting I cringe to read:

All literature taunts the time we carry on our watches.

Some devious error foisted her into that career.

Conjoined with the inward thrust of Hans' aggression stands the vitalized fear of castration.

You see why I had to become an English teacher.

Should you write active or passive sentences? Either. Both!

[3] *Revising Prose,* New York, 1979, p. 3.
[4] *On Writing Well,* 2d ed., New York, 1980, p. 102.

Each sentence you write should be the simplest and most normal way of saying what you want to say in the context in which you are writing. If you are writing about a boy's experiences, he will be the subject of most of the sentences. Thus *He was kicked by a goat* may fit more smoothly than *A goat kicked him.* If in addition you want to surprise or amuse your reader, *He was kicked by a goat* may do the job better, because its punch comes at the end.

In some contexts the passive voice must predominate. In scientific and social scientific writing, for example. Daniel Kevles, a historian of science, explains that because of

the scientific community's convention of impersonality . . . scientific papers must be written in the passive rather than the active voice. The convention essentially declares: The actors in research are much less important than their processes and results. Only the truth about nature is worth having. Knowledge of the human beings who seek it is relatively unimportant.

As for the verb *to be,* it isn't dull or wishy-washy. Quite the contrary, it is the strongest of all verbs: it asserts existence and nonexistence ("To be, or not to be: that is the question"). Moreover, though it appears in every passive sentence, it isn't a passive verb. *You are reading this book* is an active sentence. *I was a fool* is, too, though some grammarians disagree. *They are wrong.* (You see how definite the verb *to be* is. That is what makes it strong.)

Odd, energetic verbs *(gnaw, topple, sidle, kvetch)* are fine every now and then. Once in five hundred words, say. But when they appear close together, the result is, like my college writing or Zinsser's list, tiring and show-offy.

The truth is you can't avoid the passive voice and the verb *to be.* In normal writing the verb *to be* occurs in nearly half the sentences. What you *can* avoid, and should, are pointlessly passive sentences that tie themselves in knots rather than make simpler statements in the active voice. Two examples. First:

It is apparent from the article that the strength and unity that all the Woodstock goers experienced are admirable to *Time.*

Change that to:

Time makes clear its admiration for the strength and unity the Woodstock goers felt.

Second:

In today's society it is half-expected by teens to receive an automobile at age sixteen.

Change that to:

American teenagers sort of expect to get a car for their sixteenth birthday.

Don't Exaggerate. Don't Make Your Language "Entertaining." Stay Cool. Underplay

A student wrote about the allergic reaction she had to her contact lenses. Here are two paragraphs from her paper. In the first she is speaking on the phone with her eye doctor's receptionist:

"Un, yes, good morning," I lied. "This is Suzanne McDonald, and I got my contacts from Dr.—" "Thank you very much. Just a moment, please," said the disgustingly happy soprano, and for a second or so the line went dead. On hold, I groaned, and groaned again as the Muzak clicked on. What if I really were dying and I had to sit here listening to "You Are the Sunshine of My Life" playing out of my telephone? What on earth is taking them so long? Another click. Thank God, it's about time. "Susan?" You would think those people would have learned to pronounce my name by now. "We've found your file." Oh, wonderful. Maybe I can just hang on and let them lose it again. "What can we do for you this morning?"

In the second paragraph the student is speaking on the phone to her eye doctor's nurse:

I sighed. "This is Suzanne McDonald calling. I'm having some problems with my eyes. They're all red and swollen up and they hurt a little and there are some globs of white stuff kind of oozing out of the corners. I was wondering if I ought to come in or what I can do about it."

The second paragraph, which tries so little, seems to me more successful than the first, which tries so hard. The writer wants her readers to be amused. This wish leads her, in the first paragraph, to inflate her reactions. She tries to push us into being entertained by insisting on how *awful* her experience was. But readers are people: we don't like being pushed, even by language. We like having our own responses, not someone else's. Despite her loud exasperation, what the writer tells us in the first paragraph doesn't sound awful. What she tells us in the second paragraph, on the other hand, though she says it unemotionally, sounds downright alarming.

Less is often more.

Here is one of the most painful paragraphs I know. It is from John McPhee's book about frontier Alaska, *Coming into the Country.* Note that it never tries to describe what a bad toothache feels like. It simply tells us in cool, flat words, how an isolated trapper reacted to a toothache.

He lay down in his cabin and waited for the nuisance to pass. But the pain increased and was apparently not going to go away. It became so intense he could barely stand it. He was a couple of hundred miles from the most accessible dentist. So he took a pair of channel-lock pliers and wrapped them with tape, put the pliers into his mouth, and clamped them over the hostile tooth. He levered it, worked it awhile, and passed out. When he came to, he picked up the pliers and went back to work on the tooth. It wouldn't give. He passed out again. Each time he attacked the tooth with the pliers, he passed out. Finally, his hand would not move. He could not make his arm lift the pliers toward his mouth. So he set them down, left the cabin, and—by dogsled and mail plane—headed for the dentist, in Fairbanks.

When You Tell What Happens in a Poem, Play, Novel, Film, Dance, Painting, or Performance, Put Your Verbs in the Present Tense

This is the custom among writers of English: to use the present tense when describing people and events in works of art or fiction. Thus we write

Mona Lisa smiles—or does she? Some who have looked at her a long time say she is cringing before the sorrow of the world.

Hamlet impulsively draws his sword, thrusts through the arras, and kills Polonius.

As Orson Welles portrays him, the young Kane has a playfulness that hides his megalomania.

There is a logic in using the present tense because what happens in a fiction, even one written thousands of years ago, is alive to us as we read it or see it performed. It is alive to us, too, as we think and talk and write about it. In a sense Hamlet is always killing Polonius.

Lurching Adverbs

Try not to use *ly* adverbs—like *brief*ly, *clear*ly, *strong*ly—close together because they give writing a lurching sound.
Write *first, second, third* rather than *firstly, secondly, thirdly.*

Alliteration and Assonance

Try to avoid alliteration and assonance, especially of *s* sounds.
Similar sounds siphon attention from the subject and toward the words. The prose gets clotted, too chockful.
Sibilance exasperates.

Fine Phrases

Nonfiction writing will tolerate a handsome phrase every now and then.
Last Sunday, while I was reading in the Philadelphia airport, a middle-aged man came up and handed me a pen with a printed card that read:

Ladies and Gentlemen
I AM A DEAF PERSON

I AM SELLING THIS CARD TO
SEE MY WAY THROUGH

My Prayer for You Is
MAY GOD BLESS YOU
PAY ANY PRICE YOU WISH
Thank You   Good Luck

The phrase "see my way through" seems to me to work beautifully. It means, of course, "help me make a little money" or "earn a living," but it has broader connotations, biblical overtones, and it alludes to its bearer's disability in an upbeat way. It means *more* than its explicit meaning—which is just what a fine phrase must do.

Don't hesitate to try such poetic phrases

1. infrequently (used often they make writing soupy)
2. when, as here, the context will support a noble tone, and
3. so long as a broader phrase makes the basic meaning plain.

Images and Metaphors

George Orwell, one of the finest writers in our language, gives you this advice: "Never use a metaphor, simile or other figure of speech which you are used to seeing in print."[5]

My advice is different: Don't use metaphors and images when you don't have to.

Orwell didn't have to to make his point. I didn't have to to make mine. You usually won't have to to make yours.

It is true that the images and metaphors in a piece of writing may interest, amuse, baffle, disgust you and thus stick in your mind. But if the writing is nonfiction, its images and metaphors and the emotions they arouse are less important than the point being made. They are incidental diversions. The really interesting thing is, or should be, the subject.

[5] "Politics and the English Language," reprinted in *The Collected Essays, Journalism and Letters of George Orwell*, eds. Sonia Orwell and Ian Angus, New York, 1968, IV:139 [which means volume IV, page 139].

When an image gets *too* interesting and elaborate (as for example, *across his deep slow eyes there fumed a tear*), when a metaphor is too surprising (as, *barnlike dejection*), the reader's attention is turned from the subject to the language and the language-user. This is all right in some sorts of fiction, especially poetry that means to call attention to its brilliant way with words. But such brilliance weakens nonfiction writing.

The novelist Ford Madox Ford has argued that what it weakens is *narrative*, whether the narrative is fiction or nonfiction. Ford collaborated with Joseph Conrad on several novels and plays. He found that the two of them working over a passage would sometimes come up with a descriptive word, image, or metaphor that was unexpected and surprisingly *right*. When they read the passage over the next day, though, what had seemed right was plainly wrong. Their surprise stuck out of the passage in a distracting way, like a dead fish on the living room sofa. According to Ford, "*too* startling words, however apt, *too* just images, too great displays of cleverness" broke the momentum of what was being said. So Conrad and he replaced the startling words with humbler ones. "We used to say: the first lesson that an author has to learn is that of humility. He must learn that the first thing he has to consider is his story and the last thing he has to consider is his story, and in between that he will consider his story."[6]

Writing gurus who tell you to perk up your prose with lively description and figures of speech, as Jim Corder does in the passage I quote on page 31, are misleading you. What makes interesting writing is interesting content, good "story."

Having said this, I don't want you to think that I'm against images and metaphors. I'm not. I just don't want you to think you *have* to squeeze them into your writing. The writer Robert Penn Warren tells about a student who had written a nice

[6] Ford Madox Ford, *Joseph Conrad: A Personal Remembrance*, London, 1924, pp. 193–95. See also Ford's article "Techniques," *The Southern Review*, July 1935, pp. 20–35, in which he explains his goal: "to write *just* words that would not stick out of a sentence and so distract the reader's attention by their very justness."

short story, which Warren praised. The young man said,
"Oh, it's not finished yet. I have to go back and put in some
symbols."

Don't think your writing is unfinished if it doesn't have
images and metaphors. Images and metaphors will come into
your writing when they need to as unavoidably as symbols
come into fiction. While writing this book I have sometimes
found that what I wanted to say went best in an image or a
figure of speech. I have then used one. A conspicuous example of this is the last sentence of Chapter 1 (page 19). So
conspicuous it has been worrying me.

How About Conversation in Writing?

Great! Conversation breaks the monotony of the writer's
voice talking all the time. It brings in sentences that are less
calculated than written ones, more klutzy and lifelike.

"But there's a problem," you say. "I don't remember con-
versations."

Well, nobody does. You don't want a whole conversation
anyhow. Just a couple of sentences.

"But I don't remember the words," you say. "How can I
write down sentences if I don't remember the words?"

Oh, you remember the words, some of them. You got a
tape recorder? Use it.

"No."

Why not?

"I don't have a tape recorder."

Oh. Well, you do your best. You take notes. You write
down the words you remember, and you fill in other words
that give the sense of what was said.

"That's making it up!"

Shh. No, no, it's not making it up. Not the sense of it.

"But if I'm not sure a word was said and I write it down,
I'm making it up."

You're giving an honest impression of what was said.

"That's not fair."

It's *fair*. It's what people do. It's not perfect. It's fair.

Quoting

Novice writers don't quote enough conversation. Most of them, however, quote too much writing. They overquote for two reasons.

First, they are insecure and crave any support they can get. Rather than stand up, say something, and dare the lightning, they prefer lying low and letting someone else say it, or something like it. In *Historians' Fallacies* David Hackett Fischer observes that overquoting

is widespread among young scholars, who have a way of articulating a thesis in a series of quotations from older scholars and original sources—quotations which are strung together like beads on a necklace, with a few connections of their own invention. Their own best statements are sometimes buried in the notes, where nobody can find them. As historians gain maturity, they tend to become more assertive in their own right. But the habit is not easily broken.

And only when courage overcomes timidity.

The second reason novice writers quote so much is that they have been taught to. They are taught to because they are taught to write in English courses, where what one writes about, from age fourteen upward, is literature. English courses require the close analysis of literature, and this requires frequent quoting from the text in question. Here for instance, grabbed at random, is Harold Bloom's *Visionary Company* explicating part of the first stanza of Shelley's poem "The Witch of Atlas" after having quoted that stanza in full:

Mutability, Saturn's incestuous daughter, bears to her father (Kronos, or "Time" in Greek) two cruel twins, Error and Truth, Blake's "cloven fiction." These antithetical gods hunt all the "bright natures" of myth from the earth and leave nothing to be believed in, to be "worth the pains" of the "learnéd rhyme" that "The Witch of Atlas" is.

Close textual analysis—"close reading," as it is sometimes called—isn't the sort of writing most of us need or want to do once we have gotten out of English class. The writing we want to do isn't about words. It's about people, things, events —life, in a word. It is done for reportorial or social scientific or business purposes, or for our own pleasure and, occasionally, the pleasure and edification of others. In such writing overquoting clogs the narrative flow. Here is a student writing about John Foster Dulles, who was President Eisenhower's Secretary of State:

His father was a Presbyterian minister, and Dulles himself looked like one. He had a "thin face, long nose, and rimless glasses." His face had "a bitter expression" of "stern self-righteousness." He proclaimed his belief that Communism was "immoral."

We note that there is a missed transition in this passage: it glides too easily from Dulles' face to his hatred of communism. (A possible bridge: " '. . . self-righteousness.' He had a self-righteous Christian's view of communism. Communism was atheistic, and that was one reason he called it 'immoral.' ") The passage's big problem, though, is all those quotes—an infestation made worse in the original paper by the fact that each quote dragged behind it a footnote number, 22 through 25.

Let's be frank: writing that quotes writing is a nuisance for readers. Quotes take extra energy to read. A reader has to figure out who is talking, how the quote relates to what came before, why (simply) the blasted thing is there. Quotes have to be worth quoting, and most of the quotes in the Dulles passage aren't.

When are quotes worth quoting?

1. when they put words before the reader for close analysis
2. when they are crucial evidence
3. when they say something so well it can't be said better.

The second criterion justifies one word quoted in the Dulles passage. The word "immoral" is crucial evidence of Dulles' anti-communism, the intensity of which the student meant to demonstrate. According to the student (which is to say, according to the sources she cites), Dulles himself called communism immoral, surely a significant word of derogation.

The other quotes in the passage are not evidence of this sort. "Immoral" is a word of historical importance because it shows how Dulles felt. The quotes describing his face, appearance, and character are not. The facts they point to may be significant, as the student believes, but the particular words that state these facts are not. "Thin face, long nose," "bitter expression," and so on are not, *as words,* evidence of anything. Furthermore, they do not describe Dulles so brilliantly as to oblige quotation. Given five minutes and a pencil, you or I could take the facts they state and come up with a stronger word portrait.

That is what the student should have done. She should have quoted the most telling (to her purpose) things Dulles said about communism, while writing in her own words a description of Dulles based on photographs and earlier descriptions, the most useful (to her) of which she would then cite in a footnote ("My portrait of Dulles draws mainly on descriptions of him in . . .").

I'm making a distinction here that is related to a distinction you probably know: the distinction between "primary" and "secondary" sources. David Hackett Fischer speaks of young historians stringing together quotes "from older scholars and original sources." Those original, or primary, sources are words—or indeed any artifacts—created at a certain past time. Writings that later comment on those "original" words or artifacts are secondary sources, like the writing done by scholars.

Another way to understand what you should quote, then, is to say that in general you should quote primary (or original) sources, like Dulles' "immoral," and not secondary sources, like historians' descriptions of Dulles' nose and glasses. The exceptions to this general rule we have already indicated. You will have to quote a secondary source to analyze, attack, or defend it (in such a case the source becomes a *primary* source illustrating the point you are making), and you may want to quote a few words from a secondary source if it says something more brilliantly than you can. But the general rule holds: read secondary sources, rework what they say into your argument, crediting them in your text or footnotes, but don't quote them.

Look at part of the Dulles passage again:

He had a "thin face, long nose, and rimless glasses." His face had "a bitter expression" of "stern self-righteousness."

We don't believe those facts a bit more for having them in quotes. Their expression is so commonplace we don't understand why the quotes are there. We begin wondering who said them—maybe that makes them worth quoting. But here the student's description runs counter to another suggestion I'd make. She doesn't tell us *in the text* who wrote or spoke the words she quotes. To evaluate the quotes we have to go to the bottom of the page or the back of the paper. Like the quotes themselves, the trek to the sources is a waste of our energy—22: a historian. 23: a newsmagazine. 24: a politician writing as a historian. The sources prove nothing, except that the writer who quoted them was timid and wanted to impress us with the various stones she hadn't left unturned.

No:

- Quote seldom (it's you we came to hear, not someone else).
- Quote as briefly as possible.
- Quote what a participant said, not a later commentator (with exceptions).
- And, most important, quote only what is important enough to quote.

Plagiarism

Plagiarism is copying someone else's work. Because we moderns put such emphasis on originality, we think plagiarizing very bad and punish it hard. I am not saying we are right to do so: I am only saying we do it. Fair warning.

There are at least three kinds of plagiarism. The first and most obvious happens when one writer copies another writer's words without crediting the source or putting the words in quotation marks. Jeffrey Meikle, my colleague in American Studies at the University of Texas at Austin, has found the following:

Benjamin Quarles, *The Negro in the Making of America,* New York, Collier, 1964, p. 77:

Many slaves struck out alone and unassisted. Some who, despite the laws, had become literate made use of passes and "free papers" they had forged. Some, with nothing but the North Star to guide them, took to the woods, walking by night and lying in swamps by day, covering themselves with leaves.

Robert Goldston, *The Negro Revolution,* New York, Macmillan, 1968, p. 83; New York, Signet, 1968, pp. 79–80:

Many slaves made their way north with the aid of passes and "free papers" which they had forged. But most, with nothing but the North Star to guide them, took to the woods. They would travel by night and hide out in caves or holes during the day, taking the most unlikely routes—preferably through swamps.

Goldston uses many of Quarles' words, but he doesn't put them in quotes or cite Quarles as their author. His book has no footnotes; its bibliography doesn't include Quarles' book, though it includes *other* books by Quarles. Presumably Goldston intended to credit Quarles' work and somehow neglected to. The result is, I think, plagiarism.

The second sort of plagiarism is less obvious. A writer copies what another writer has said by paraphrasing a passage without crediting the source.

Quarles, *The Negro in the Making of America,* p. 71:

The lot of the typical slave, regardless of locale or occupation, was influenced in large measure by the psychological and legal controls brought to bear on him. All slaves were inculcated with the idea that the whites ruled from God and that to question this divine-right-white theory was to incur the wrath of heaven, if not to call for a more immediate sign of displeasure here below. A slave was told that his condition was the fulfillment of the will of the Master on high; catechisms for the religious instruction of slaves commonly bore such passages as: . . .

Goldston, *The Negro Revolution,* Macmillan, pp. 69–70; Signet, p. 68:

While propaganda was relied upon to keep poor whites in line, the controls brought to bear on slaves were not simply those of overwork and the lash. There were legal and psychological controls also. One of the most favored was religion; but this was sometimes a two-edged weapon. Masters made sure that Sunday sermons included repetition of the idea that whites derived their right to rule over blacks from God. To question this right was to question the will of God and incur divine wrath. Catechisms for the instruction of slaves in the Christian religions often contained such passages as: . . .

Whether or not it is intentional, such close paraphrasing without giving credit I consider plagiarism.

The third sort of plagiarism is still less direct. Words aren't copied or paraphrased, but an idea is borrowed with no credit given. You remember Student X's paper. You also may remember my saying (page 23) that after I read the paper to X's class two other students wrote papers saying the same thing. Because those writers didn't credit Student X, they were plagiarizing—innocently, to be sure, since they knew I knew the source of their idea.

This sort of plagiarizing is difficult to avoid. Philosophers and psychologists say that there are no original ideas, that we can only have ideas, or modify ideas, other people had before. No doubt true. It is also true that we are constantly saying things which come, adapted or straight, from people we now forget. (Who for example are the "philosophers and psychologists" I just didn't name? Wish I knew.)

Nevertheless, here's the test. If you know who suggested an idea you are using, you need to give them credit. That's fair play. Otherwise, you are plagiarizing.

As I mentioned, the Quarles and Goldston passages quoted above were noticed by Jeff Meikle, who used them in an explanatory page on plagiarism he wrote for his students. Jeff concluded the page:

To avoid plagiarism, enclose all direct quotations in quotation marks and cite your source in a footnote. Avoid direct paraphrasing. Instead redevelop whole paragraphs and arguments in your own words. And even then, cite your sources or source in a footnote. Work hard to place facts within your own personally developed framework. Have something to say. Then you won't find yourself repeating what someone else has said. As insurance, in case you are questioned about plagiarism, save all notes, outlines, and drafts used in the writing of each paper.

Is It All Right to End a Sentence with a Preposition?

Yes. And to start one with an *and*. Or an *or*.
But not a *but?*
On the contrary, *but* is a fine word to start a sentence with. Just as *with,* a preposition, is a fine word for ending a sentence. It is also fine to brazenly split an infinitive when a sentence sounds better that way. Some of the old prohibitions are dead.

How Long Should Your Sentences Be?

Journalism researchers have found that the average English sentence written and published today has eighteen words in it. Of course averages vary from periodical to periodical and book to book: sentences in scholarly quarterlies average more than eighteen words, sentences in supermarket tabloids average less. But eighteen is average.

Some composition teachers argue that writers ought to be aware of how many words they put in their sentences and keep a rough balance between short and long sentences. Why? For rhythm.

Richard Lanham is an exponent of this view. In *Revising Prose* he condenses and rewrites a wordy paragraph into the following: "Prose will seem sincere if it seems credible, but how credible will depend on who reads it. A scientist, for example, would welcome a candid statement of alternative views." Lanham is satisfied with his revision:

We've taken this passage about as far as it will go, but one problem still remains. The rhythm seems okay (try it, as always, by reading it aloud with emphasis and coloration), but both sentences run to about the same length. For this reason, the one which follows this passage ought to be either much longer or very short.[7]

Nonsense. The next sentence should be the length it needs to be to say what it means to say. No longer, no shorter. You don't write a sentence to get a certain rhythm. You write to say something.

Say Things Once

Say things once. If you want to say something more than once, say it—but as you're saying it, *add* to it. Don't simply repeat.

(When you repeat yourself, tell your readers you are doing it. They will then know that *you* know what you're doing and that you aren't trying to slip the same information by them again as something new.)

Student writers repeat themselves because they are afraid they won't be understood. "That numbskull teacher," they think. "Will he understand this? I better say it again." With consequences like the following, from Student YY:

The chief problem I have with my writing is that I'm unable to clearly express myself on paper. In other words, I cannot clearly tell the readers what I'm saying.

In other words? But that first sentence was perfectly clear. It didn't need to be rephrased to help us out.

Here's from another school theme:

The Egyptians are extremely interesting to us today for various reasons. Modern science would still like to know what the secret ingredients were that the Egyptians used when they wrapped up dead people so that their faces would not rot for innumerable cen-

[7] Pp. 12–15.

turies. This interesting riddle is still quite a challenge to modern science in the twentieth century.

This paragraph is a fine parody of teenage writing. It is the essay Holden Caulfield writes for his prep school history teacher in J. D. Salinger's *The Catcher in the Rye.* Holden is a great repeater of the obvious—"My brother Allie had this left-handed fielder's mitt. He was left-handed"—and the reason he repeats himself is the reason many young people do: insecurity. He is afraid his readers won't understand him, as indeed the people in Salinger's novel usually don't understand him.

Have you Holden's paranoia? Do you think people don't understand you? You may be right: in real life they may not. But people understand you when you write. Even if you write incomprehensibly, they understand you ("He's a terrible writer. Boy!"). And when you actually *say* something in writing, people understand it even if you only say it once. Even teachers understand it, though they may pretend not to or may complain about the way you express yourself. What readers don't understand is the repeating of something. "Why is he saying that again?" they wonder. "What does he take me for—a numbskull?"

It is important that readers not feel that you are writing down to them. They may not know as much about the subject you are writing on as you do (we hope they don't), but they are not idiots. John Fischer, the former editor of *Harper's Magazine,* believed that one of the hardest things for a writer to learn is to write for readers who are uninformed without treating them as unintelligent.

Saying something once means more than eliminating redundant sentences and phrases. Seen bigger, it is a principle of organization—Dwight Macdonald's "great basic principle": say everything you say on a subject at one time. Seen smaller, it is a test for every word in every sentence. Does this word need to be here? Does it add something? Does it add enough?

Do you think it impossible to look skeptically at every word? It's not. Begin with the "doublets," the paired words. Are both really needed? *A dull and boring play:* couldn't it just be *dull* or *boring?* If it's one, we understand it to be the other. *Her behavior and attitude puzzled and confused me.* Couldn't we say *Her behavior puzzled me* or *She confused me?*

Try to have no more doublets per page than you can keep well separated—three at most. Here are three in a sentence:

During the permissive and committed sixties the values and life style of the young exercised an unprecedented influence over Western culture and traditions.

"Permissive and committed" is a nice compound of contraries. But the other doublets should go:

During the permissive and committed sixties the values of the young exercised an unprecedented influence in Western culture.

Since you're going to say things only once, you've got to say them right: briefly, clearly, and strongly.

One Way to Tell if Your Sentences Stink

Read them aloud. If you can do this without getting tangled in the words and without embarrassment, the sentences are probably good.

What to Do When a Sentence Stinks

Change it.

How? Easy. Read a stinky sentence over. Figure out what it means. (If you can't figure out what it means, write a new sentence and try to figure that one out.) Now do as V. S. Pritchett recommends (see page 79): put the sentence's meaning in your own words. Try the first words that come to mind because they are likely to be the most natural. Putting the meaning simply and in common words you may have to expand the sentence into two or three sentences. That's allowed. When you have rephrased the sentence, discard the original sentence and keep the rephrasing.

What if the rephrasing, though an improvement, is still pretty rotten? Change it. Start the process over. Rewrite the rewritten sentence even more plainly. Keep simplifying it until you wouldn't be embarrassed to say it aloud to your parent or a frowning stranger.[8]

We all write sentences that are awful. There is nothing to do with such sentences but rewrite them. But when you recognize that you have written a bad sentence, there is no reason not to improve it. Recognizing a bad sentence is half the battle. That done, all it takes to write a competent sentence is the wish to, patience, and practice.

Writing, as the cliché has it, is rewriting.

Unfortunately the way we are obliged to write in school doesn't suggest this. We have to write forty-minute in-class themes or answer essay questions on tests. Such assignments, made to order for good writers, do not develop a useful skill. In life it is astonishing how rarely you are given half an hour to write a thoughtful essay on a topic.[9]

There *is* writing you can do quickly and thus should do quickly when you want to. This writing is either very informal—like a letter to a childhood pal—or very formal—like a memo to Maintenance requesting that the heat be turned up in your office. Because this writing is either so free form or so

[8] You may of course imagine the Respectable Other you write for any way you like. Tolstoy saw his preferred reader as a clean old peasant; the poet W. B. Yeats, as a "wise and simple" fisherman with freckled face and gray Connemara suit.

[9] Students are given little at-home writing for reasons that make life easier for the teacher. (1) An in-class essay means the teacher doesn't have to teach a class. (2) An at-home essay naturally grows longer and more complex than a classroom essay and hence takes more time and ingenuity to grade. Writing done at home can be carefully done, which makes a moral demand on the teacher for a careful evaluation, whereas writing done in class must be slapdash, which allows the teacher's response to be also. (3) At-home writing is more likely to fall under parental purview and thus raise questions as to what and whether the student is being taught.

In fairness to teachers, it should be said that correcting and commenting on student writing is terrible work. I would rather mop the floors than do it. In fact the two jobs are similar.

formulaic, it is easy for most people. Those with secretaries learn to dictate it.

But this sort of writing we are not called upon to do in school. (We ought to be. It would make us more confident with language.) Rather, we are called upon to do writing that takes reflection, invention, careful and unprecedented articulation. Such writing can't be done in a few minutes.

The belief that writing comes fast, comes as it is shown in the movies—a pen racing words across the page; a typewriter chattering madly, thrown to the side, chattering again—is a Romantic fallacy like inspiration, which, as someone must have said, is the world's first excuse for doing nothing. Most writing comes slowly. It is more like painting a wall than driving a car. Be patient with your writing. Be patient with yourself. Remember: you are not prisoner to the first thing you write down. Or your first revision of it. Or your second.

Below are some bad sentences with my suggested revision in parenthesis. The first sentence was by a freshman:

We have become a generation of children who have acquired a loosening grasp on the english language.

(Our generation is losing its grip on English.)

A hitchhiker explains his method:

Many people when they see your sign it tells them whether they have to go out of their way if they pick you up.

(Your sign tells people whether you would take them out of their way.)

A young political commentator:

Many Americans today feel a sense of bewilderment that could be lessened by a surfacing of leaders who feel an obligation to direct.

(Many Americans today feel a sense of bewilderment that could be reduced if leaders came forward who felt an obligation to lead.)

A young historian:

[G. David] Shine, by being drafted into the Army, brought [Roy M.] Cohn's rage on that service.

(The Army enraged Cohn by drafting Shine.)

From a paper contrasting "living together" and marriage:

Marriage is not meant to be a puppy-love paradise that involves only peace, love, and happiness, but to many people this is what they believe.

(Marriage is not meant to be a puppy-love paradise of peace, love, and happiness, but many people believe it is.)

The same paper:

Fortunately I think that a relaxing of social pressure to be married and a better education have led to less mistakes or at least to find out a mistake before too much damage is done.

(I think there is fortunately less social pressure to be married these days. That and better education have led to fewer bad marriages— or at least to quicker and less painful divorces.)

A student plays my message back to me:

Nobody wants to read something that won't exchange information and insight for a better understanding.

(People want to read writing that tells them something.)

Put Words in a Sentence Where They Sound Most Natural

Syntax is the placement of words in sentences. Good syntax is putting words where native speakers of the language would put them.

Syntax is one thing not to be creative about. Don't fight the obvious; give in.

Earlier he will come.	[awkward syntax]
He earlier will come.	[awk syn]
He will earlier come.	[syn!]
He will come earlier.	[right]

A Strong Sentence

To make a sentence strong, try putting its most important word at the end. (As I did in that sentence.)

This doesn't always work—nothing always works. But it works often enough to be worth mentioning.

Slow the Flow

Because inexperienced writers believe they can write fast, they write fast. The result is writing like this by Student ZZ:

The chief problem I have with my writing is that the sentences sometimes become too long and confusing. I am often not sure where to cut-off one sentence and begin another. When I write my thoughts seem to flow in a continuous stream. I then just put my ideas on the paper. Thoughts often come so quick I can't write fast enough or I already know the next sentence. I would like to write without stopping. This is probably not a very good style because I shouldn't expect people to understand the way I think. My problem is planning sentence structure. I need to stop at the end of each sentence and consider what I've said. If I would ask myself is it clear to the reader I'm aware of the fact that to best convey your point you must state it as simply as possible so it can be easily understood. I myself often get bored with short undescriptive sentences. I like lots of adjectives and verbs. My mistake is in trying to make the sentence exciting and colorful to catch the reader, rather than simple and forceful. Vocabulary fascinates me and I love to exercise it whenever possible. A mistake along the same line of my basic problem; simplicity.

An interesting performance. Student ZZ means to commit the faults he criticizes. He is willing to do this because he knows the faults are real and wants help in correcting them. More power to him.

Writing like ZZ's is usually criticized as "choppy" because it shifts from topic to topic, or muddles them together, without transition. (What sort of transitions are missing? How about the simplest: "In the first place . . . ," "Then too

. . . ," ". . . also . . . ," "But . . ." and a paragraph break or two?)

The writing is choppy and should be smoothed with transitions, about which I will speak in a moment. But I want now to say something else about it.

It is frenzied. It is written at a pace so breathless that control is impossible.

A significant portion of the writing we teachers see is like this. Such writing is tough to improve because it isn't really bad in any one place: it's bad throughout. Its approach is wrong. To be made better it needs to be rewritten at a slower tempo.

I may be particularly sensitive to this kind of bad writing because I used to do it on essay tests. Rather than state an idea and prove it, I would dump on the page everything I knew about a subject, trying to show how much it was. Rather than *answer* the question given me, I would do what ZZ does here: *wallow* in my topic, thrashing my arms now in one direction, now in another, faster, faster. My handwriting would jumble, scrawl, and finally disintegrate on the page. Saying everything, I was saying nothing and hating what I said, disagreeing with it, knowing it was crap, knowing that whoever read it would learn just one thing: my desperation.

The way to stop doing such frantic writing is to stop doing it. Write slower. Don't try to put on paper the flow of your ideas as they come to you—they move too fast. Instead, create for your reader a new flow of ideas, each one examined in all the detail it needs before you move on to the next. Keep that flow so slow that anybody can follow it.

Transitions

"Awk trans" . . . "Trans?" . . . "We need a trans."

The student wanted to ask a question about these comments I'd made on her paper. "I'm sure you're right," she said, "because another teacher said the same thing."

I told her I wasn't sure I was right. "Some people like more transitions than others," I said. "Me for example: I like a lot of transitions. So when I say you need transitions, I'm probably suggesting you put in as many as I would. Or nearly."

"Un-huh," she said, nodding, looking at me. Then she popped the question. "What's a transition?"

Glad she asked that.

1. Transitions are words like *so, but, on the other hand, first, in addition, however, nevertheless, thus, for example* that change or channel the direction in which a subject is being treated.
2. A transition is a sentence like *I am now going to talk about baseball* or *footnotes* or *something else* that announces a new subject.

If you change the subject you are writing about or your point of view on a subject without giving the reader a transitional word, phrase, or sentence, the reader may be exasperated or lost, as some readers may have been by Student ZZ's paragraph on page 126.

Incidentally, don't be afraid of using simpleminded transitions like *I will now discuss A* or *In order to understand A's relation to B, we must first understand B.* Tell your readers where you are and what you are doing; lead them with confidence, and most will follow. They will follow because they want to feel in touch with you, the writer. They don't want to be lost—as readers often are (E. B. White estimates that readers are lost half the time).

I now want to propose a third, more general way of understanding what a transition is and does. I don't know that other people think of transitions this way, but I do and find it helpful.

3. A transition is anything that links one sentence—or paragraph—to another. Nearly every sentence, therefore, is transitional. (In that sentence, for example, the linking or transitional words are *sentence, therefore,* and *transitional.*) Coherent writing, I suggest, is a constant process of transi-

tioning. Just as I believe in continuous organization, I believe in continuous transitioning.

A page or two back I suggested that you slow the flow of your sentences. Having now defined a transition as anything that links sentences together, I suggest further that you . . .

Link Your Sentences Together to Smooth Their Flow

Here is a paragraph from a student paper:

Any MASH viewer knows that despite acting and writing changes, the theme of war as insanity has remained constant. Even when Dr. Hawkeye Pierce fades into an episode's background, we see events from his viewpoint. To Hawkeye, there is nothing noble about the American presence and purpose in Korea (and, by extension, of course, in Vietnam). War to him is a sick game played by heartless, self-glorifying officers.

Notice how the first sentence puts forward one subject and the second puts forward another, apparently unrelated. The two subjects *are* related, but we don't know this until the *third* sentence, which is a sentence late. We don't know it because there is a transition problem: the sentences aren't doing their proper linking job. The student should have put enough of the third sentence into the second sentence to make plain the second sentence's relation to the first. For example:

Any MASH viewer knows that, despite acting and writing changes, the theme of war as insanity has remained constant. Dr. Hawkeye Pierce loathes war with a bitter, laughing loathing, and even when he isn't at the center of an episode, we see things from his viewpoint. To Hawkeye, there is nothing noble about the American war in Korea (and, by extension, of course, our war in Vietnam). War to him is a sick game played by officers.

You see my reason for doing this. You see also that I have changed "the American presence and purpose in Korea" to "the American war in Korea" because *war* is the linking keyword that knits the paragraph together, and *presence and purpose* is too vague a synonym for it.

May I ask you now to reread the original paragraph?

Thank you. Did you notice the bump between the first and second sentences? No? Look again.

Now please reread the revised paragraph.

No bump. Tying the sentences together smoothed it away. You can smooth the bumps from a paragraph by continuous transitioning.

You can smooth the bumps from a paragraph, but you usually can't from *between* paragraphs (though I just did it here).

You usually don't want to.

You want a bump between paragraphs.

Wakes the reader up.

Paragraphing

How long is a paragraph?

As short as that.

Shorter.

Or as long as it needs to be to cover a subject. The longest paragraph in this book may be the 336-word one on Winston Churchill's "We shall fight . . ." speech (page 84).

When the topic changes, a new paragraph starts.

But there is a complication. Writing that aims to be inviting, like the writing in newspapers, popular magazines and books, uses shorter paragraphs than more ambitious and "profound" writing. New paragraphs are begun before a topic is exhausted.

Anytime.

For no reason at all.

Because each new paragraph lightens the tone, encourages readers, offers a foothold down the page.

When paragraphs are short, writing does seem easier. Less happily, it also seems disjointed and superficial—as though the writer can't concentrate on a subject.

Thus paragraphing, like so much else, is a matter of tone. You want to have a proper paragraph length for your subject, your audience, and your degree of seriousness (or frivolity).

The magic word!

Have you noticed, though, we haven't come across it yet. Why not? Books on writing, books like this, are often called style books because they assume each of us has or wants a style to express our individuality, and they give advice on how style can be acquired.

Peter Elbow, in his style book *Writing Without Teachers,* tells the reader:

In your natural way of producing words there is a sound, a texture, a rhythm—a voice—which is the main source of power in your writing. I don't know how it works, but this voice is the force that will make a reader listen to you.

That is comforting, but I don't think it's true. I think readers listen to what you say, not to some mysterious force in your voice.

William Zinsser, in his style book, *On Writing Well,* says:

Ultimately the product that any writer has to sell is not his subject, but who he is. I often find myself reading with interest about a topic that I never thought would interest me—some unusual scientific quest, for instance. What holds me is the enthusiasm of the writer for his field.

I don't remember ever reading about a dull subject just because the writer was excited by it. I think the ultimate product that writers sell is what they say, not who they are.

I think most style books are built on a false premise. I don't think style generally shows individuality—not if the style is literate. I don't think an "individual" style is something to be concerned about or to cultivate, unless perhaps you are writing fiction or poetry. Further, I'm no longer sure I know what style is. I don't know that anybody knows. A magic word indeed.

I try to pay attention when people talk about style because I think their use of the word may clarify its meaning. In *Poison*

Penmanship Jessica Mitford reprints three of her articles about American funeral customs. She then comments for several pages on the writing of the articles and the reception they got. Among her comments are the two paragraphs that follow:

A word about style. Rereading the first two of these pieces, I note that I did somewhat tailor the writing to what I perceived as the readership. For the *Satevepost* with its alleged circulation of ten million—always an inhibiting thought to me, those millions of faceless folks!—I see that I adopted a plonking one-two-three approach, setting the scene for the reader with a number of rather obvious rhetorical questions, and proceeding from there to my eminently logical (if self-serving) answers as furnished by the response of the American public to my book *[The American Way of Death]*.

The piece for *Nova,* then a trendy English glossy mag, is a good bit more relaxed. The clergy have virtually disappeared to be replaced by cocktail party talk. The Nancy Mitford reference, the young English friend who answered my letters, the generally chatty and personal tone would hardly have struck the right note for the *Satevepost.*

Mitford says she will talk about "style," but what she actually talks about is better defined by other words. In the first paragraph she uses "style" to mean *method, organization, strategy, approach* (she uses the last word). In her second paragraph, "style" means *tone* (she uses this word).

I agree with Mitford. Style has many vague meanings, but its two most definite ones are *organization* and *tone.* Since these words have precise meanings I recommend using them in place of "style" at every opportunity.

As for "individuality" of style, I have trouble putting my hands on it. Look at what you read. Newspapers, for example. Is there anything "individual" about the writing in the news reports? Of course not. The editorials? Consciously not. The syndicated columns? Sometimes *maybe.* George Will writes brisk sentences on the right, while Anthony Lewis writes mild sentences on the left—but certainly each man's "style" tells less about him than his views do. Most columnists can only be told apart by their beliefs and their bylines.

Can you tell Ann Landers from Abigail Van Buren? By their *prose?* And even if their prose were different, what does the difference tell you about each woman's "individuality"?

Look at a magazine you read regularly: *Time, Good House-keeping, The Economist, Playboy, Mad, True Confessions, Scientific American*—it doesn't matter what. Within the magazine is there much difference between the style of one article and the style of another? No. To be sure, *among* these magazines there are many different styles, tones, types of writing, ways of winking at the reader. But once a magazine's editors decide who their readers are and the tone that best will reach them, those who write for the magazine adopt that tone. If they don't, they don't get published, or the editors adjust their copy to the tone (which is sometimes miscalled the "house style"). It isn't difficult to translate a piece of writing into another tone: Russell Baker's parody of "Little Red Riding Hood" (page 80) was less funny than it meant to be just because the translating he did was so obvious.

Or look at this book. You have been reading me for 133 pages now. You know what most of my ideas on writing are. What do you know about me as an individual? Am I liberal or conservative? Smiler or frowner? Spendthrift or scrooge? Am I good with children (do I have any?) and other small mammals? How fast do I drive? Do I believe in an afterlife?

Pages and pages of my style haven't told you.

Now, it is true that some great writers have recognizable individual styles. Sometimes the style is good, like Ernest Hemingway's ("In the fall the war was always there, but we did not go to it any more"). Sometimes the style is bad, like Theodore Dreiser's ("The 'death house' in this particular prison was one of those crass erections and maintenances of human insensitiveness and stupidity principally for which no one primarily was really responsible"). Sometimes a great writer writes both well and badly in his individual style, as Hemingway and Dreiser did, and Vladimir Nabokov, William Faulkner, and Henry James. But writers with idiosyncratic styles, good or bad, are few. Many great writers don't have one: for example Saul Bellow, George Orwell, E. M.

Forster, Thomas Hardy, George Eliot, Hawthorne, Dickens, Cooper, Scott, Fielding, Defoe. Most popular writers don't: stylewise A. Haley, author of *Roots,* is indistinguishable from A. Hailey, author of *Wheels.*

Moreover, as I've already suggested, an individual style doesn't necessarily tell us anything about the individual who created it. Robert Frost's poetry has a strong personal style, a product of its friendly tone. Yet in his personal life, most witnesses agree, Frost was a nasty man. The only artist I've known, Walker Evans, made photographs celebrated for their aloofness (when he took a snapshot of my daughter, Walker told her, "Look sad!"). In his personal life, by contrast, Evans was warm, intense, restlessly curious. Whatever it is, style has no necessary relation to its author's character.

For, contrary to what we are told, style is impersonal. Style is lily-gilding. Except in "art" writing—and often even there —style doesn't matter much. Compared with content, style is nearly always trivial. So when you are told to think about style, especially an "individual" or "personal" style, you are getting bad advice.

Here is my advice:

Don't think about style. Instead, think about writing clearly and simply, and saying what you want to say as strongly as you can. Don't try to *write with style.* Write plainly.

If someone tells you your writing lacks style, nod and say you were never able to figure out what style is. If someone tells you your prose is dull, say, "My apologies. But you understood what I was saying?" If, however, someone tells you your writing is unclear or your content dull, ask them why. And press them for an answer. It may give you a great deal to think about.

A LATER NOTE.

I have been given a great deal to think about.

You may remember my telling you that an editor, before agreeing to publish my manuscript, would have it appraised by several experts in the teaching of composition. This has happened, and the experts—anonymous to me—have made recommendations that helped me make many improvements in the book you are reading.

One expert, who advised against publishing the manuscript, pointed to this section as an example of the "insufficient help" I give.

Stott tells readers not to worry about style, just to write as simply as they can. Supposing they can't write simply? That is the problem throughout: he doesn't tell readers *how* to become better writers; he merely expects them to do so.

The expert may be right. If so, I apologize, reader. If not, I apologize anyhow. I have tried to give you tips on how you can write simply (use simple words, use short sentences, use person-words as sentence subjects, write as you talk, etc.). But I know how tough it is to listen to advice for as long as you have been listening to me and then to realize that your problem still isn't answered and won't be answered however much you read, because the problem can only be answered by you, not by some blabbermouth in a book.

Like every other how-to-write-book writer, I have been sailing under false colors. I have encouraged you to think I can make you write better. Not true. Only you can make you write better. The most I can do is give you some ideas that may help you rethink the way you write.

Which doesn't mean I'm going to shut up—anymore than I shut up when friends and colleagues and editors and anonymous experts disagreed with or were indifferent to much of the stuff I liked best in my manuscript. I'm going to do now what I did then: try to say better what I really want to say.

The expert thinks you may not know how to write simply, reader. I think if you can't, you can learn to, as I learned to.

The trick (not that it's a trick) is to forget about impressing anybody with the way you write—forget, that is, about style. Concentrate instead on what you want to say. Try to say it as briefly as it can be said, and in the commonest words.

After you write something, look at it. Ask yourself, "Do I really mean this? As I say it here? Every word? *That* word?" If you don't, make changes and ask the same questions of your revision. Then ask: "What I'm saying, can I say it more clearly? Is *that* word necessary? Couldn't I use an easier word? Does this sentence contribute enough? Can I say it shorter?" Make changes again. Read the passage over a few hours or days later, asking the same questions and making new changes. Keep doing this until you find you are not making any more changes.

I believe this is what you have to do to make your writing as simple as it can be. But the method (if it is a method) begins, I repeat, with a conscious renunciation of fanciness, of "style." You have to decide you are willing to be judged by nothing more than what you have to say. It takes many of us a long time to make this decision. We have to overcome our insecurity. We have to learn self-acceptance.

I wish you luck, reader. It's taken me twenty-five years to stop hiding behind words and start telling the truth from time to time. I trust you will do much better.

A STILL LATER NOTE.

I find that Matthew Arnold, the verbose Victorian poet-critic, has reduced what I say on style to four blunt sentences:

People think I can teach them style. What stuff it is. Have something to say and say it as clearly as you can. That is the only secret of style.

Writing May Be *LESS* Difficult Than You Think

I just read a student paper on two Tennessee Williams plays. It was written in the vague, twisted language of the browbeaten bad writer. Of the leading character in *Night of the Iguana* it said: "He loses his hope of reascension to the priesthood by searching for his answer in a cheap motel with an underage girl." My comment on the paper was this:

You put up a hard fight, which I admire, but you don't get beyond what is explicit in the plays. More important (for our present purposes, at least) your language defeats you. Writing is, I feel sure, Mr. J., *less* difficult than you make it. Don't "write" so hard and heavy. Write less. Write simpler. Write as you talk. "He can't be a minister anymore because he was caught shacked up in a motel . . ." Then you'll see that what matters *isn't* the words, because they are as simple and ordinary as possible, but what you're saying, which must not be simple.

Writing Versus Typewriting

Should you submit your writing in longhand or typed? Typed, by all means. I don't care how bad your typing is, it is preferable to your handwriting. For two reasons.

First, we are so accustomed to our handwriting that it is like a part of us. "Most people enjoy the sight of their own handwriting," said the poet W. H. Auden, "as they enjoy the smell of their own farts." Even if we can't enjoy our handwriting—and we may recognize that it's grubby and indecipherable—it is so familiar that we read it in a state of quasi-somnambulism. Typing wakes us up, divorces us from what we've written, objectifies it. Auden again: "Much as I loathe the typewriter, I must admit that it is a help in self-criticism. Typescript is so impersonal and hideous to look at that, if I type out a poem, I immediately see defects I missed when I looked through it in manuscript." Typing what we write makes it easier to *see* and thus perhaps improve.

Second, people write more comments on typed pages than on handwritten ones. It is easier to write them because there is usually more room in the margins—but this isn't the main reason more is written, I think. The fact is, it's hard to read a page in longhand as something other than a private letter. One skims across it, reluctant to get too close (it isn't from a friend, after all—has one the right to read it?). One's comments seem less intrusive on typed pages.

I find it helpful to type a rough draft as I go, paragraph by paragraph. I type up a paragraph when it seems close to final form in longhand or when, as often happens, I'm stuck and can't finish it and want to see it with fresh eyes.

A Tip on Typing Your Final Draft

Humorist Dorothy Parker once said the only thing she learned in college was that if you spit on an eraser it will erase ink.

Actually it won't; I've tried it. It makes a mess.

Forget erasers. Since Parker's day, Liquid Paper has been invented. (The person who invented it was a secretary; she may have been tired of spitting on erasers.) Here's a tip less flashy than Parker's, but one that works.

If you are permitted to hand in a photocopy of your final typed copy in place of the final typed copy itself, use Liquid Paper to make corrections and changes as you type. When you photocopy the final copy, the photocopy won't show what the Liquid Paper covers (of course) and also won't show the white blotches of Liquid Paper, however gross.

Word Processing

This section is an afterthought. I am writing it after everything else in the book.

A publisher has agreed to publish my book, but the editor who went to bat for it insists that I add a discussion of word processing.

"Your readers are interested in what you think of word processing," he said.

"I haven't mentioned it," I said.

"Yes, but you're going to. Have you done any word processing?"

"A little."

"Good. Maybe you should do some more."

"That's not what my book's about."

"Bill, your book is about how people write and how they can write better. Many people now write on word processors. Many more will. Your readers are going to wonder if your advice holds true for word processing."

"Well," I said, "writing is writing."

"I trust that isn't *all* you have to say." He gave a laugh.

"I hope so—I mean I hope not. I'll have to think about it. Where do you want me to talk about word processing?"

"Throughout the book, I think—a sentence here, a sentence there."

I swallowed. That would mean reworking the entire manuscript. "I could stick a section on word processing in Chapter 4."

"That might do. Give it a try."

Word processing (murky term) is done on a word processor. A word processor has four parts: (1) a typewriter keyboard connected through (2) a computer to both (3) a TV screen, which displays what is typed, and (4) a printer. Using a word processor, you can type something, change it as much as you like on the TV screen—which is often referred to as a CRT (cathode-ray tube) or a VDT (visual display terminal)—and then have your final revision typed or printed on paper without retyping a word of it.

Word processing can save huge amounts of secretarial labor. Once a text is recorded, the word processor can type it up, altered or not, as many times as anyone wants. My English department has to send out hundreds of letters of rejection to people who want to teach for us. Word processing makes it easy. A secretary types into the word processor the necessary commands, the text of the letter, and the applicants' names and addresses. The word processor gives back a stack of freshly typed letters, each with the same text but a different applicant's name and address and the appropriate salutation ("Dear Ms. Gaines:", "Dear Mr. Madison:"). Accompanying each letter is the addressed envelope to put it in.

The larger the text to be processed, the greater the potential saving. Many film writers have gone over to word processing because they can make the extensive revisions their collaborative art demands and get copies of the redone script without waiting for the whole thing to be retyped and paying $2.50 a page for the work. Say a film writer has named a character Brunhilda, and the producer wants her named

Midge. The word *Brunhilda* appears in the script a hundred times. No problem. The film writer turns all those *Brunhildas* into *Midges* by typing one four- or five-word command. Every place in the text where Brunhilda appeared, Midge replaces her. Two hours after ordering the change, the producer has the new script incorporating it.

If you spend a lot of time retyping your writing, you may decide a word processor is worth the expense. My colleague Suzanne Buckley is thinking of buying one because she finds it hard revising typescript: as soon as she pencils in a change on a page, she has the urge to retype the page. Though she fights the urge, she often loses. "I spend days typing practically the same thing over and over," she says. A word processor would give her a revised page right away.

Word processors have another virtue. They can help with proofreading. A word processor with a special program will flag misspelled words and suggest correct spellings. A few word processing programs can spot simple grammar and punctuation faults, like some I talk about in Chapter 5.

Does word processing help you *actually write* better? Some people think so. William Zinsser, in his recent book, *Writing with a Word Processor,* says this:

> Seeing is the key to writing. What the word processor could do is to revolutionize the way we think about words by displaying them for our consideration and giving us an instant chance to reconsider them.[10]

Perhaps—though it hardly seems revolutionary that a word processor lets us see the words we write after we have written them. A pen or pencil does that.

Does Zinsser mean that word processing may do what I said typing did: help writers see their words more objectively? This seems to be true for some people. Film writer Hal Dresner *(Zorro—The Gay Blade)* told a reporter:

> I have trouble rewriting when it's in my own typewriter. But being one step removed on the computer made it seem like surgery on

---

[10] New York, 1983, p. 26.

someone else's work. I could tear it to ribbons. The words seemed less permanent.[11]

Zinsser and Dresner are talking about ease of revision, not composition. Peter McWilliams, author of *The Word Processing Book,* believes that easier revision will lead to easier composition. "Once one becomes accustomed to the ease with which changes are made on word processors," he says,

it becomes easier to write more and more, take more risks, go for ideas first and perfection later. It is not a magic wand, and we do not overnight become James Joyce, or even Jack Kerouac, but, given time, a freeing of expression does take place.[12]

I noticed a freeing of expression the few times I've composed on a word processor. Frankly it scared me. When I was writing something trivial—a letter or a memo—I word-processed okay. But when I was writing something I cared about and struggling (as always) to clarify and tie together my ideas, the results were a shambles. The word processor made writing so easy I found myself letting all sorts of nonsense slip through my fingers. I think I felt compelled to *keep up with the machine* by writing as fast as it throws letters on the screen. I said things that were increasingly reckless, irrelevant, personal.

This made me think that word processing may indeed revolutionize writing. It may encourage vast, unbuttoned autobiography of the kind (yes!) Kerouac wrote, or Henry Miller. When you're seated at a word processor it takes little energy, even energy of will, to let thoughts float upward from your gut, through your fluttering fingers, onto the deadpan screen. Zinsser noticed when he started composing on a word processor "the words seemed to spring out of my fingers onto the screen." He implies that writers feel abnormally *close* to those words on the screen—"silken phrases that you are spinning, spider-like, out of your innards."

So I found. Far from being detached from what I wrote (as

[11] Quoted in Aljean Harmetz, "Computers Enter Hollywood Picture," *New York Times,* June 18, 1983, p. 17.
[12] 5th ed., Los Angeles, 1983, p. 93.

Zinsser elsewhere suggests), I felt it came from deep in me. I think a word processor may facilitate communication with one's inner self because the external distractions of writing are reduced: no pencil or paper to hold on to, no scratching across the page, no struggle of penmanship, no clanking type-writer (the keyboard makes gentle, plastic clicks), no worry about margins, no carriage return (the sentences can run on forever, stacking themselves in print-perfect rows), no misspellings, no fear of typos.

"Freeing of expression" may be the word processor's great gift to writers. For some people, word processing may be a safe, cheap substitute for drink, drugs, and dictation. It may be the ideal vehicle for "free writing" (see Appendix B). But freed expression isn't the same thing as good writing and doesn't necessarily lead to it.

"Do you write better on a word processor?" I asked my friend Lisa Beyer, a reporter for the Austin *American-States-man* and former editor of the University of Texas' student newspaper, *The Daily Texan*.

"I couldn't say," Lisa said. "Either way, writing demands the same discipline: tons of rewriting.

"I can get my thoughts down much faster with a word processor. Which has advantages and disadvantages. You sometimes find you are writing without thinking. You're rambling, you're too casual, you're introspective, you're risqué.

"So you have to go back. Chop away. Revise and edit. But that's so much easier to do on a computer.

"For me, writing on a typewriter is more serious. Because that's the way *writers* write—you know, Hemingway and the boys and girls in the attic. Also, the writing looks much more *final* on paper than it does on a TV screen. And it's much harder to get rid of.

"Even when I write on a word processor, I do a lot of editing on paper. I pull a hard copy to look at and make changes. You see different things on paper than you do on the screen. Maybe if you write *both* ways you write better."

Proofreading

No escape: you have to do it.

There are good proofreaders and the rest of us. The good proofreaders may be able to tell us how to proofread better, but nobody has told me. Yes, come to think of it, somebody tried to. She told me to look for errors in the corners of the page. "They tend to collect there," she said. My errors don't; at least the ones I find don't. They are all over.

I proofread everything I hand in three times, minimum. The first time I read it slowly, correcting the mistakes I see and making sure no words were dropped or added in the final typing. (I'll tell you how to make corrections in a moment.) The second time I try not to read it: just to *look* at the words one by one. This is hard to do: I always catch myself reading. (Much harder is what the real pros do: they read each page *backward*, bottom to top and right to left, examining each word and punctuation mark in momentary isolation from its context.) The third time I photocopy the paper (basic rule: never give away your only copy of anything you've worked on) and proofread the photocopy, which has the advantage of looking somehow like a different paper. Then I hand in the photocopy. I expect there to be errors left.

You may be like me and find it hard to proof your own writing. You get so accustomed to the sound of the sentences you have trouble seeing the words. You need to do what I try to do: find someone to proof what you write (perhaps in exchange for your proofing what he or she writes). When a publisher agrees to do this book, I am going to get it in the contract that the copyeditor will proof the galleys. (Many publishers don't spend money on proofreaders any more. Galleys are read by the printer, who doesn't want to see mistakes, and by the author, who often can't.) In addition I'll enlist co-workers, family, and friends to read proof. Nevertheless a few typos will squeeze into the book (in my last book a *big* came out *bit*). Apologies in advance.

When you see an error or a word, phrase, or sentence that

can be improved in your typescript, change it. Some people are so proud of a clean typed page they won't make improvements. A few neatness nuts won't even correct typos. This is crazy. Beside correctness, neatness counts as nothing. Handing in pages with handwritten emendations only shows you are serious about your writing.

Here's how to make corrections. Pick up a pen or pencil (I use a black ballpoint pen). If your typescript has

- An extrra letter, do this: "an extr̶a letter."
- An extraa letter, do this: "an extraa letter." Or this: "an extraa letter."
- A letter missng, do this: "a letter missᵢng."
- A litter wrong, do this: "a lᵉtter wrong." Or this: "a lᵉtter wrong."
- A letter wrongly Capitalized, do this: "a letter wrongly ¢apitalized."
- A letter that should be capitalized (freud), do this: "freud." Or this: "F̶reud." Or this: "F̶reud."
- Letters revesred or reversed words, do this: "letters reve̶s̶red or reversed/words."
- A word you don't don't want, do this: "a word you don't don't want." Or this: "a word you don't ~~don't~~ want."
- A word or missing, do this: "a word or‿missing." **words**
- A word you want to supplant, do this: "a word you want to ~~supplant~~." **change**
- Two words runtogether, do this: "two words run together."
- Too much s pace, do this: "too much s‿pace."
- No period where the sentence ends, do this: "sentence ends." Or this: "sentence ends." Or this: "sentence ends."

Editorial Help

I have just invited you to have someone read your writing and point out errors in it. Maybe this is the place to ask whether you should have someone read your writing and *improve* it.

My answer is yes, if you want to and find someone you trust. As I said earlier, publishing writers rely on editorial help of all kinds. Why shouldn't unpublished writers?

Of course if you are a student you have to ask your teachers whether they will allow you to receive editorial help with your writing. Some teachers believe such help is plagiarism (but it isn't—so long as you acknowledge the help) or unfair to the other students (but they can get help too).

I've had lots of help with this book, from people I'll name later on and people, like the anonymous experts, I can't name. My feeling is that those of us who want help saying what we have to say ought to get it.

Endings

I've spoken and will speak again of ways you end a piece of writing. You already understand, though, that you must do it as you think best, there being no Perfect Way.

When do you end? The textbooks say to do it when you have said everything you have to say. This is impossible because one always has more to say. You end, I suggest, when what you would go on to say is markedly less important than what you have already said. You end, that is, just before diminishing returns set in.

I used to try to end papers with the best thing I had to say. I now have doubts that people get to the end of what they read (you always excepted, reader) and so put my strongest points up front. As a consequence, I must take care to stop while I am still saying worthwhile things.

Someone has said that there are only two sorts of endings, the fanfare *(da-da!)* and the dying fall *(plub-plub-plew)*. It's true. You can try to avoid these alternatives by cutting your writing off abruptly—ending it without an ending so to speak. But this sort of ending is also a kind of dying fall. Dying fall endings are more subtle and various than fanfares because all fanfares sound alike. But don't be squeamish about using a fanfare when one seems warranted.

This ending is a dying fall.

5
A RUN THROUGH THE RULES

This is the last chapter in the book. It tells you how to avoid common writing faults. It tells you how to punctuate, footnote, make a bibliography, and follow parallel construction. It gives you my opinions on these matters. All this is much less important than what we have discussed so far. And more usual. This book has argued that worthwhile writing says things people haven't heard before. In one classroom or another you have heard 90 percent of what this chapter says. It's tough to be original when the subject is grammar.

By *grammar* I mean—to quote Webster's Third New International Dictionary—"a study of what is to be preferred and what avoided in the inflections and syntax of a language." In plainer words, grammar, as I discuss it here, is "good" and "bad" usage, the current rules of standard written English as I understand them.

What is standard written English? It is the variant of English used by most educated speakers of the language when they write. Is it better than other sorts of written English? Some people say yes, some people say no. All we need to say here is that it is sometimes different, and people who don't obey its rules risk appearing poorly educated.

Does this chapter give you all the rules of standard written English? Certainly not. There are far too many. Further, many of the rules—like the rule about agreement between subject and verb *(he was* instead of *he were)*—are too well known and obeyed to need repeating. Many other rules aren't worth knowing or obeying. In John Barth's novel *The End of the Road,* Jacob "Jack" Horner, the hero-villain, a teacher of grammar, announces to his freshman English class,

Predicate complements of infinitives of copulative verbs without expressed subjects go into the nominative case, whereas predicate complements of infinitives of copulative verbs *with* expressed subjects go into the objective case. "I was thought to be *he,* but I thought John to be *him!"* Questions?

Yes, why would you want to remember a rule so trivial?

The rules I'm going to talk about here are the ones that give writers frequent and important difficulty. I estimate that violations of these rules account for 75 percent of writing faults other than misspellings.

This book has argued that such faults don't matter much. I have said you can be a good bad writer and write well while writing incorrectly. But just because good usage doesn't matter much doesn't mean it doesn't matter. Let's not kid ourselves: it does matter.

The Period, the Sentence, and the Fragment

The period is the most useful punctuation mark. Be sure you use it enough. When I am having trouble with a sentence, I often find I'm trying to squeeze too much into it. It needs to be *two* sentences. Or three.

Make your sentences as short as you can while still saying what you mean to say. As a general rule, the shorter the sentence, the stronger it is.

Novice writers have been told this, but many don't *feel* it to be true. They underuse the period because they don't like ending sentences. They think long sentences are the hallmark of real writing. Their sentences waffle on, the commas trying to do the work of periods and semicolons in mazes like the following:

Both are photographs of swimming pools, the first by Liz Kohl, entitled *Diamond Shamrock Houston,* is a picture of the pool at the Shamrock Hilton taken at night with the lights on, nobody there swimming as is usual then.

Several short sentences would be preferable to this.

We know that a period goes at the end of a sentence. It also goes at the end of a sentence fragment. This, for example. (Or this.) Consider the following passage, which has an incorrectly punctuated sentence fragment.

Pick up your first issue of *Your Own Magazine.* (on sale now at newsstands everywhere) It won't be your last.

That is wrong.[1] This is right:

Pick up your first issue of *Your Own Magazine* (on sale now at newsstands everywhere). It won't be your last.

So is this:

Pick up your first issue of *Your Own Magazine.* (On sale now at newsstands everywhere.) It won't be your last.

And this:

Pick up your first issue of *Your Own Magazine* (from a newsstand— where else?).

Teachers have told you to write "complete" sentences, with subjects and verbs and, usually, predicates. (In the preceding sentence, the subject is *teachers,* the verb is *have told,* and everything else is the predicate.) Teachers may have graded you down for writing a sentence fragment ("frag") or a "NAS" (not a sentence) like "On sale now at newsstands everywhere." This is foolish and pettifogging, provided your sentence fragment was clear in its context. Here is the writer Thomas Thompson:

---

[1] By "wrong," here and hereafter, I mean that something doesn't obey the rules of standard written English.

Forty-three years later, on a broiling summer noon in 1974, Mrs. Rhea Robinson sipped the thick chicory coffee of her native Louisiana and remembered the long-ago adoption. Or, at least, her version.

Here is the critic Susan Sontag:

All that photography's hidden program of realism actually implies is the belief that reality is hidden. And, being hidden, is something to be unveiled.

Here is the London *Times'* tennis correspondent:

There were times when [Björn] Borg's anticipation was such that he seemed to attract the ball to his presence. Times when his speed and deft racket control, especially on the forehand, challenged belief.

Here is a freshman student:

For four years I hitchhiked inside the Green Bay city limits. I had no problems getting rides; in fact, I was quite successful. So successful that my friends called me the "platinum thumb."

In all four examples the last sentence is a fragment.

These fragmentary sentences are fine—every bit as good as "complete" sentences. When are fragments *not* fine? When they interrupt the logic and momentum of a passage by leaving something out. Here's the same hitchhiker, same paper:

The rewards of hitchhiking are numerous. The obvious reward is getting to your destination cheaply. Secondly, the cross section of people.

Yes, what about it? Another freshman:

I like to learn a lot. Considering that paper we did about problems we had writing.

Oh, you learned a lot from that?

To put it simply: fragments are fine so long as they make as much sense as full sentences would.

Words in Italics and Other Special Words

This is roman type. *This is italics.* Italics are used to set words off from the rest of the text and show they are special.

When you write in longhand or type on a standard typewriter you can't italicize words because you don't have a second, different-looking typeface to use. Therefore, to make your reader understand that you intend a word to be italicized, you underline it. If your writing is later set in print, the compositor will take the words you have underlined—as, <u>The Grapes of Wrath</u>—and put them in italics—as, *The Grapes of Wrath*.

Italics have three main uses:

1. To indicate that words, though in an English sentence, belong to another language:

From Brownsville south along the Mexican coast, the cormorant is called *pajaro burro,* or donkey bird.

Many words and phrases that come from other languages are now accepted as English. For example: amok, bizarre, esprit de corps, frankfurter, gestapo, guru, kamikaze, nirvana, ski, status quo, vis-à-vis, voodoo, zombie. Such words appear in our dictionaries with no notation that they are foreign. They should be used without italics:

Enchiladas and sauerkraut are de rigueur.

2. In titles, like the following:

The Grapes of Wrath	*The Economist*
Antigone	*What's Up, Tiger Lily?*
The New York *Times*	Dakar *Matin*
Mozart's *Requiem*	the *Titanic*

Though many titles are italicized, many are put in quotes:

A Hard Day's Night [the film]
A Hard Day's Night [the record album]
"A Hard Day's Night" [the song]

How do you know whether a title should be put in italics or quotes? Here is a simple answer. Things that are big and that take a long time to happen are usually italicized, while things that are small and brief are quoted. Thus the names of ships, planes, statues, books, films, plays, records, radio and TV programs in a series (as, *Star Trek),* newspapers, magazines, operas, symphonies, and ballets generally go into italics, while the names of poems, short stories, songs, articles, essays, chapters, bulletins, handbills, one-time radio and TV programs (as, *Star Trek's* episode "City on the Edge of Forever"), paintings, drawings, and photographs go into quotes.

In fact, though, there is a good deal of flexibility on this matter, particularly as regards works of visual and performing art, and most publications and publishers make their own rules about what to italicize, what to quote. I say all the following are fine:

Swan Lake	"Swan Lake"
"Mona Lisa"	*Mona Lisa*
The Thinker	"The Thinker"
"Yes, We Have No Bananas"	*Yes, We Have No Bananas*
Mork and Mindy	"Mork and Mindy"
Keats' "To Autumn"	Keats' *To Autumn*

3. To emphasize particular words:

The truth will *never* be known.

I want to say more on this last point. There are three sorts of punctuation commonly used to emphasize particular words. The first is italics:

We are considering a *social problem.*

The second is aberrant capitalization:

We are considering a Social Problem.

The third is unattributed quotation marks:

We are considering a "social problem."

Each of these ways of punctuating words changes their meaning.

Italicizing underscores a word's meaning, tells us to take it seriously. A *social problem* demands our concern. To say someone writes *well* is praise indeed.

Aberrant capitalization makes light of a word, tells us it isn't As Important As It Pretends. When presented in capital letters, a Social Problem or the Desire to Write Well are transformed into matters of interest only to stuffy fools. This sort of Playful Capitalization has become popular, I think, thanks to A. A. Milne's children's stories about Winnie-the-Pooh and Milne's most influential disciples, the Bright Young Things who wrote *Time* magazine in its early years. Such capitalizing shows the reader how superior the writer is to the subject. In the spring of 1981 British television began *Gay Life,* a documentary series about homosexuality; a *Sunday Times* reviewer wrote of the first program: "The series, and this film, on lesbians, is definitely a Good Thing, but is somewhat simplistic and didactic." That sentence has the habitual tone of the Aberrant Capitalizer: such-and-such is good for the poor dears who don't know any better and who *need* it, but for the rest of us . . . well, it's a little primitive.

Putting a word or phrase in unattributed quotation marks can do several things.

1. It can apologize for the word, either because it is vague

He had a nice "heavy" quality

or because it is slangy and vulgar

She loved to play the "bohunk."

2. It can warn us that the word is being used in an unusual way:

Auto "Walks" on Water.

3. It can call the word in question. In his introduction to *The Communal Experience: Anarchist and Mystical Communities in America* Laurence Veysey explains how he chose the communities he studied:

I wanted to choose groups which in each case would represent a given alternative (past and present, this-worldly and other-worldly, structured and unstructured) at its "best." This selection of groups of each kind at their "best" seemed appropriate if the aim was to give the communitarian tradition the maximum opportunity to display its importance and potential. But what does "best" mean?

Exactly. Who says it's "best"? "Best" by what standard? To put a word in quotes and not say who said it asks the reader to question the word and who it belongs to.

Similarly the writer who calls a social problem a "social problem" has decided it probably isn't one. Someone else thinks it is, but the writer urges reconsideration:

Children playing ball in the street is not a "social problem," as Mr. Cutting thinks. It is amusement. The social problem is lack of proper space for such amusement. Children (adults, for that matter) should not have to play ball amongst cars, parked or moving.

4. It can criticize the word—even reject it. In *A Death of One's Own*, the story of her husband's battle with cancer, Gerda Lerner writes,

The authority of the doctor expert is given to him entirely by the patient's free consent, and yet patients all too often forget their rights once they put themselves "under" medical care.

The quotes around "under" attack that word. Why, Lerner is asking, do people dealing with doctors put themselves in the subservient relationship that word implies?

As the columnist William Safire has noted, this use of quotation marks means to say "somebody else's word, not mine." Often it also means to turn the quoted word into a sneer. During the writing of this book an international incident called forth millions of sneering quotation marks. Fifty-two American diplomats were held hostage in Teheran from November 1979 to January 1981 by Iranians who called themselves students. When it became clear that the Iranians spent their school days terrorizing the hostages and blackmailing the U.S. government, the American media turned the word *students* against them by putting it in quotes. "Students"—it became a curse word, spat out. "So you call yourselves 'students,' " said the media. "In a pig's eye."

The Comma

The comma has more uses than any other punctuation mark. Here are the main ones, from simple to intricate. Use commas:

1. To set off words of direct address from the rest of a sentence:

Hey, Mr. Tambourine Man, play a song for me.

No problem here, eh, reader? We put commas around the object of direct address—"Mr. Tambourine Man" or "reader," you—to show that it isn't part of the syntax of the sentence. There could be confusion if it were. Without a comma the film title *What's Up, Tiger Lily?* becomes a question for a physician.

2. Between comparative statements like *The bigger they are, the harder they fall.* Tolstoy:

The more we live by the intellect, the less we understand the meaning of life.

3. To separate numbers in dates: July 2, 1776. Note that a comma isn't needed when only month and year are given—December 1910—or when numbers are separated by words in the date—12 March 1983.

4. To set off words of interjection from the rest of the sentence. What are words of interjection? Well, the *well* at the start of this sentence is one. And so, in similar contexts, are *yes, no, eh, hey, hell, alas, oh, huh, okay, please, all right, boy, sure, you know,* and other conversation fillers. Of course an exclamatory interjection may be followed by an exclamation point:

Hot dog! Now you're talking.

5. In place of omitted words:

Proofread everything you hand in three times, minimum.

The omitted words here are *at a.*

Rebecca read all or most of seventeen books; Neal, one.

The omitted words here are *read all or most of.*

"A teacher is to teach, not to judge"—Maria Montessori.

The omitted words here are *and* or *A teacher is.*

6. To set off a direct quotation that is independent of the sentence introducing it.

She said, "All is nothing." "Not at all," he replied. "Well, if it's not," she said, "I'd like to know what is."

Note that when quoted words are *part* of a sentence they are not set off by commas:

"Guided democracy" was the name Sukarno gave his dictatorship.

Signs saying "Stop" cost less than traffic lights.

The reviewer called the film "adorable trash."

Many people have the idea they must throw down a comma whenever there is a quotation mark. Definitely not. The commas in the following sentences are wrong and should be omitted:

She praised his talk as, "very stimulating."

"Food and furry friends," are promised on the picnic.

Politicians are currently discussing, "the stagflated economy."

7. Between two or more items in a series when the items (words, phrases, clauses, or short sentences) are not separated by *and, but, nor, or,* or *yet.* Thus:

> French or Greek or Russian
>
> on land, on sea, in air
>
> stately, plump Buck Mulligan
>
> an infuriating and hilarious foul-up
>
> It wasn't skill, it was dumb luck.

Note that in a series that uses commas the comma before
and, but, nor, or, or *yet* is optional. "Eeny, Meany, Miney, and
Moe" could be punctuated "Eeny, Meany, Miney and Moe."

Note also that though a comma is often put between two
verbs separated by *and, but, nor, or,* or *yet* ("compound
verbs," as they are called) it is not necessary there. The following sentence appears on London theater tickets. The su-
perfluous comma I find an impediment to the sentence's
meaning:

Tickets cannot be exchanged or money refunded unless a performance is cancelled, or abandoned when less than half the performance has taken place.

Note finally that adjectives in a series don't take commas
when they precede the noun they modify and work together
to form an indissoluble unit with it:

> a traditional Indian summer rain dance
>
> twelve angry young men
>
> that little old red schoolhouse

So indissoluble are these units, you will notice, that you can't
put an *and* between any of the adjectives, as you could in the
phrases "stately, plump Buck Mulligan" or "twelve angry,
hairy young men."

8. Often, though not always, after introductory words,
phrases, and clauses:

Since I have but one life to live, let it be as a hang glider.

Furthermore, most people are happy ignoring the problem. [Or:
"Furthermore most people are happy ignoring the problem."]

After the concert, it began to rain. [Or: "After the concert it began
to rain."]

To write something new and useful, you must know the context in
which you are writing. [Or: "To write something new and useful
you must know the context in which you are writing."]

This comma is generally optional. Use it when you think the reader might have trouble unearthing a sentence's subject from the stuff you have put in front of it. Here is the London *Times:*

In the biggest and most bitter of Wall Street takeover battles, the Du Pont chemicals company has increased its offer for Conoco to counter a higher bid by Seagram, the Canadian distiller.

In fact, the comma after *battles* could be omitted with no harm done. The only time harm is done is when confusion results.

When he left Pittsburgh fought hard and tied the score.

That sentence needs a comma after *left.*

9. Often, though not always, around words, phrases, and clauses used transitionally—words, phrases, and clauses like, for example, *however, nevertheless, though, anyway, incidentally, first, again, frequently, in fact, of course, more important, for example, on the contrary, needless to say, if you follow me, according to conventional wisdom, as we saw in Chapter 3.* Such words are put in sentences to guide readers, point their attention. Frequently the words are used to start sentences. (Needless to say, some writers would put a comma after that "frequently." And some writers would leave out the comma after that "needless to say.")

How do you decide whether to put commas around a particular transitional word, phrase, or clause? By the context and by ear.

He did not therefore look at the article.

He did not, therefore, look at the article.

Either is fine. Which way does the sentence sound better to you, given what comes before and after it? Try reading it aloud. If the *therefore* makes you pause and drop your voice, it probably needs a comma.

And not *one* comma: two. Many people these days forget to close their transitional words on both sides. Here's a freshman:

It seems then, that if something makes one feel guilty and morally offended, indeed it must be unjust.

No. If there is a comma after *then,* there has to be one before. If there is a comma before *indeed,* there has to be one after.

10. Often, though not always, between independent sentences joined by the words *for, and, nor, but, or, yet,* or *so* into compound sentences:

The modern musical begins with either *Show Boat* or *Oklahoma!,* and Oscar Hammerstein 2nd wrote them both.

There are several things to be said about this comma. In the old days, which aren't so long ago, not to use it was a serious fault. Today many people leave it out when the first sentence is short and many newspapers and magazines leave it out even when the first sentence is long (did you miss it in this sentence?). This is a comma you can go easy on if you're concerned about overpunctuating.

Writers learn to go easy on it because they see it clogs the flow of the second sentence when that sentence begins with a word, phrase, or clause that also needs commas. Here is Margaret Mitchell, *Gone with the Wind* (New York, 1936), page 904:

Never before or after did the names Republican and Scallawag carry such odium, for now the corruption of the Carpet bag régime was at its height.

Since there's no problem with clogging, Mitchell puts a comma before *for.* Now look at Mitchell's next page, 905:

The mismanagement of the state road especially infuriated the taxpayers for, out of the earnings of the road, was to come the money for free schools.

By the rules, *for* should be surrounded by commas. But that would be heavy and punctilious, not the tone Mitchell wants. She drops the comma before *for,* trusting—no doubt rightly —that the introductory phrase *out of the earnings of the road* and the commas around it will adequately warn readers that they have moved into another sentence.

Or consider this, *Gone with the Wind,* page 953:

India [Wilkes] lived with Aunt Pitty and, if Pitty sided with Melanie, as she wished to do, India would leave.

Again, the scrupulous might make it:

India lived with Aunt Pitty, and, if Pitty sided with Melanie, as she wished to do, India would leave.

But if you don't like either of these options (and the first is somewhat misleading and the second, clunky), there is another possibility, which I think I'd choose:

India lived with Aunt Pitty, and if Pitty sided with Melanie, as she wished to do, India would leave.

All of which shows that the conjunctions *for, and, nor, but, or, yet, so*—acronym: FAN BOYS—give a writer some flexibility in the punctuating of compound sentences. But the FAN BOYS are privileged words. They can join two independent sentences together with, or without, a comma. Other words, even other conjunctions, can't do this. Students keep thinking they can:

I tried and tried to figure things out for myself, because I couldn't I turned to Harvey for some medicine to cure the illness in my golf swing.

When I finished painting I knew I had to clean my brush, nevertheless I forgot to do it until I unfortunately found some gasoline in a coffee can.

The use of commas before *because* and *nevertheless* in the above examples is what is called a "comma fault" or "comma splice." Each comma should be changed to a period or a semicolon.

11. Often, though not always, around supplemental words, phrases, and clauses—which is to say, words, phrases, and clauses that supplement or qualify a sentence's meaning but that could be omitted and still leave the sentence making sense. Such words, phrases, and clauses are italicized in the following sentences:

The Du Pont chemicals company has increased its offer for Conoco to counter a higher bid by Seagram, *the Canadian distiller.*

Thin and twisted, the sound of a flute wandered across the lake.

Robert, *who needed it,* got the job.

English teachers explain these commas with a barrage of big words. They say the stuff in commas is "parenthetical." (But if it's parenthetical, why isn't it in parenthesis?) They speak of it as "appositives" or "words in apposition," as though all appositives belong in commas (they don't). Or they say it is "nonrestrictive" rather than "restrictive," and half the students invert the meaning of the two words before they leave the classroom, it being logical that a "restrictive" word, phrase, or clause go in commas, where it would be *restricted,* and this being, alas, backward.

So let's try again. You remember I quoted two of my students' sentences on page 27 and said that the commas in them were "grammatically wrong and shouldn't have been used." Let's see why. Here is sentence A:

A. One thing few people realize about the new television show, *Mork and Mindy,* is that it is one of the top five most watched television shows in America today.

Why shouldn't the phrase *"Mork and Mindy"* be in commas? It's an appositive, after all. It plays the same grammatical role in the sentence as the phrase it qualifies, "new television show."

True. But in sentence A *"Mork and Mindy"* doesn't qualify or add to the meaning, it *is* the meaning. It isn't supplemental information: it is essential. A new TV season had started, and there were dozens of new shows, *Mork and Mindy* just one of them. To speak of "the new television show" didn't sufficiently single it out—it had to be *named.* And the writer meant it to be named. That is the sentence's meaning: *Mork and Mindy* is one of the five most popular TV shows in the country. So when the writer put commas around *"Mork and Mindy"* and thus implied that the show's name was only extraneous information, he was false to the meaning he wanted the sentence to have. To make sentence A's grammar correspond to its meaning—that is, to make it grammatically *correct*—both commas must be removed:

One thing few people realize about the new television show *Mork and Mindy* is that it is one of the five most watched programs in America.

But say the writer had written the sentence another way. For example:

Few people realize that a new television show, *Mork and Mindy,* is one of the five most watched programs in America.

How about that, reader?

Answer: that's fine. But *different.* The writer's meaning here is not the same as his meaning in sentence A. Here he is saying that a new TV program is one of the five most popular. The program's name, *Mork and Mindy,* is incidental, supplemental information (as it is in *this* sentence). Such information generally goes in commas.

Or consider sentence B.

B. It hasn't been widely recognized that Woody Allen's movie, *Love and Death,* which takes place in early 18th century Russia, implies that society is a big joke.

This sentence would be fine if Woody Allen had made only one movie. The writer's meaning would then be: it hasn't been widely recognized that Woody Allen's film, his only film, the title of which, incidentally, is *Love and Death,* implies . . .

But Allen has made many films. Because he has, *"Love and Death"* is essential information, and the first comma in sentence B needs to be removed. The *second* comma, after *"Death,"* should remain because it introduces the supplemental clause *which takes place in early 18th century Russia,* which belongs in commas. Thus:

It hasn't been widely recognized that Woody Allen's movie *Love and Death,* which takes place in early 18th century Russia, implies that society is a big joke.

What if the writer had written

It hasn't been widely recognized that Woody Allen's "Russian" movie, *Love and Death,* implies that society is a big joke.

Would that be okay?

Yes. The word "Russian," or any other adjective pointing to a specific film, would change the writer's meaning. He would now be talking about Allen's "Russian" or "1975" or "seventh" or "first historical" or "third Cinemascope" or "best" or "worst" film, and the film's name would become extraneous information. The sentence would make perfect sense without it.

Note, however, that the adjective must single out a specific film. If the writer wrote "Woody Allen's funny movie *Love and Death*" he would use no commas because Allen has made other funny films. Similarly he would use no commas in the phrase "Woody Allen's typically overrated movie *Love and Death*" since the phrase "typically overrated" doesn't point to *one* film—indeed asserts there are several such films.

Most comma mistakes are made with this comma-around-supposedly-supplemental-material. And most of the mistakes are not of omission. Very simply, commas are used where they have no business being. A student:

Disco has been made popular by the famous 1977 film, *Saturday Night Fever.*

Take out the comma: *Saturday Night Fever* wasn't the only "famous" 1977 film. Another student:

My friend, Donna Given, has a dog that brings home jogging shoes.

Ms. Given's not your only friend—take out the commas. Two students this year:

John Steinbeck's novel, *The Grapes of Wrath,* . . .

Take out the commas. Steinbeck wrote sixteen novels. Five students in the last three years:

John Ford's movie, *Grapes of Wrath,* . . .

The commas don't belong there: Ford made about 130 movies.[2] *Newsweek* magazine's gossip column:

Lynn Redgrave, 38, called a press conference to complain that Universal Television wouldn't let her breast-feed new-born daughter Annabel on the set of the series, "House Calls."

House Calls isn't the only TV series: take out the comma before its name. A front-page story in the Austin *American-Statesman:*

The tallest building in the area, it resembles a transplanted Houston skyscraper, a monolith with a window pattern that's earned it the sobriquet, "The computer card."

Never mind the quotation marks. That sobriquet is essential information, so take out the comma (". . . earned it the sobriquet 'The computer card' "). A UPI dispatch about a vigil protesting an execution in Nevada:

The crowd also carried candles, prayed in unison and sang the hymn, "Amazing Grace."

If they sang *a* hymn, it's "Amazing Grace" preceded by a comma. If they sang *the* hymn, it's "Amazing Grace" unimpeded (". . . sang the hymn 'Amazing Grace' ").

I find the British have as many problems with this comma as we in America do. Henry Fairlie in the London *Times:*

The American literary and social critic, C. Hartley Grattan, noted in 1932 that . . .

Take out the commas around "C. Hartley Grattan"; even in 1932 America had more than one literary and social critic. The Lord Chamberlain, 24 February 1981:

---

[2] A complication. In one context the phrase "John Ford's movie, *Grapes of Wrath,* . . ." is correctly punctuated. Say we are writing a comparison of Woody Allen's movie *Love and Death* and Ford's movie *Grapes of Wrath.* We announce this topic, then discuss Allen's movie for several pages, then start a new paragraph, "John Ford's movie, *Grapes of Wrath,* . . ." This is correct punctuation because readers already know which Ford movie we are going to discuss. The title *Grapes of Wrath* is there to remind readers, not inform them; as supplemental, inessential, information it belongs in commas.

It is with the greatest pleasure that the Queen and the Duke of Edinburgh announce the betrothal of their beloved son, the Prince of Wales, to the Lady Diana Spencer, daughter of the Earl Spencer and the Honourable Mrs. Shand Kydd.

The Queen and Duke have two other sons and presumably love them too. Remove the commas about "the Prince of Wales."

Hang in there, reader! I've come to the last thing I want to say about commas. There is an idea current, promoted by lazy teachers and energetic linguists, that because commas usually mark a pause in speaking they should be put wherever there is a "natural" pause in a sentence. This is not true. The assumption that a comma goes anywhere it *sounds* like there's a comma, clutters our writing with commas as awkward and baffling as the comma in this sentence.

Consider the following. A student:

How such a community could vote all one way, demands an answer.

A British student:

A person who is declared legally competent, has the right to die.

The local superintendent of schools in a letter to taxpayers:

One of the most essential influences on a child's school achievement level in school, is the degree of interest and concern of his or her parents.

The Economist:

But the ferry's high cost and steadily declining number of passengers, cannot be cured by government subsidy.

A 1983 Ford advertisement:

What is needed in a time when people are keeping their cars longer, is a car people can be proud of longer.

The comma in each of these sentences doesn't belong there. It calls attention to the wait between subject and verb —exaggerates it, stalls our forward motion. We find ourselves

at the end of a pier, the departing boat too far to step to—
then are shoved forward and fall on the moving deck.

I suppose we could concoct a rule to take care of this interruptive comma. We could say that seldom does *one* comma go
between a subject and a verb *(two* commas, of course, often
go there). But this is a petty rule, if it's true enough of the
time to be considered a rule. (Here's an exception to it:
"Those who can, do. Those who can't, teach.") And I don't
think more and smaller rules are what we need, reader.

This is a fine time to say so, I realize—just when our book
has gotten dogmatic and begun laying down laws. Nonetheless I do say it. We don't need to load our minds with trivial
rules, which we then comb the countryside for applications
of. Much better to teach ourselves to have the patience to
read what we and others write—*really* read it, read it just as it
is there before us—and ask of it commonsense questions like,
what does it mean? why is it said thus? could it be said simpler? Teach ourselves, for instance, that when somebody
writes "a child's school achievement level in school," the
phrase really is as redundant as it sounds—like speaking of a
mountain resort in the mountains—and that one of the refer-
ences to school should go (leaving, "a child's achievement
level in school" or "a child's school achievement level").

The pointless comma is a particular nuisance when it comes
between subject and verb because it breaks the sentence before anything gets said. But it appears many other places. The
poet Carl Sandburg:

I can remember many years ago, a beautiful woman in Sante Fé
saying, "I don't see how anybody can study astronomy and have
ambition enough to get up in the morning."

Sandburg was writing words he was going to speak on the
radio, and maybe he put the comma after *ago* to remind himself to pause before the warm words at the heart of his sentence, its direct object, *a beautiful woman.* Nevertheless, when
he came to put his sentence in a book he should have added a
comma after *remember,* thus setting off the whole phrase *many
years ago* as a piece of extraneous information ("I can remem-

ber, many years ago, a beautiful woman . . ."), or else taken
out the aberrant comma after *ago*.

Mickey Spillane in the first of his Mike Hammer thrillers,
I, the Jury:

I chose a book that had a lot of pictures. It was titled, *Psychology of a
Marriage.*

Spillane may have tossed in the comma because he felt he
needed one before quoted material, which is what he may
have considered the book title. I suspect, however, that he
was misled by the fact that in speaking one takes a little pause
before titles to show vocally where the sentence leaves off
and the title begins.

Certainly it was this pause that misled the copywriter who
composed the text for a sign beside a reconstructed dinosaur
in the Dallas-Fort Worth Airport:

About 70 million years ago, this Plesiosaur swam the seas where
now stands, the Dallas-Fort Worth Airport.

The comma after *stands* is a honey. It means to be a Pause for
Effect in recognition of the airport's grandeur. Instead, it
makes the airport seem so inconsequential the writer forgot it
and had to take a breath before he or she remembered just
what *was* there on the brown flat land.

Today's mail offers another pointless comma, in a fund-
raising letter from a Senate liberal:

Each year the sun beams to our planet earth, 28,000 times more
solar energy than all the commercial energy used by mankind.

Don't trust pauses. They aren't necessarily commas. When
there isn't a reason for a comma—and I've given the important reasons here—don't use a comma.

The Dash

The dash does two things. It interrupts a sentence—like
this—or extends a sentence—like this.

The information that a dash introduces is brief, exemplary,

explanatory, or extraneous. Sometimes it is a little surprising. The title of a long-running London comedy: *No Sex, Please— We're British.*

The dash—why I don't know—almost makes us hold our breath. It is the only genuinely excited punctuation mark. (The exclamation point's excitement is phony! It tries too hard! We know it's pretending!) That is why the dash is handy for shifting gears in mid-sentence:

She did her own writing—but always sent telegrams.

The creative people make the difference—and not just those who happen to write well.

When a dash extends a sentence, the extension itself may be a short sentence—this is an example. In the eighteenth and nineteenth centuries a dash used thus was often preceded by a comma. The architect and antiquarian Sir John Soane (1753–1837) wrote this prayer to his dead wife:

Dear friend, I can no longer hear your voice,—tell me what I must do to fulfill your wishes.

Today we consider the comma after *voice* unnecessary. The dash is strong enough to bridge the sentences alone.

Indeed, when a dash and a comma come in the same place, the dash takes precedence and expunges the comma. The oral historian Studs Terkel wrote this blurb comment for Ronald Fraser's recent book, *Blood of Spain:*

Ronald Fraser, in going to the source itself—the flesh-and-blood survivors—has stunningly captured the feel of the Spanish Civil War.

Logic demands a comma after *itself* to complement the one at the start of the phrase *in going to the source itself.* But the interruptive dash before *the flesh-and-blood survivors* swallows up the second comma.

English teachers tell you not to overuse the dash. This is because many dashes give a page a choppy look and a gushy tone. When I find I have dashes in adjoining sentences, I try to revise one set out, unless of course I'm trying for parallelism. Glancing over the pages of this book, I see that I seldom use dashes more than twice a page, often less. Examples apart, I've used dashes only once in discussing the dash here (third paragraph, first sentence).

Incidentally, typewriters don't have a dash on them. What they have is a hyphen: -. To make a dash when typing you must type *two* hyphens--thus.

The Parenthesis

A parenthesis is a whispered aside to the reader (like this). It is an offstage voice giving information unavailable in the main text (the secret word tonight is SECRET). It is a wink across the footlights, an index finger wagging for the roving camera (hi, Mom).

Parentheses encourage us to believe the information they contain is franker and more direct than what is in the main text. A recent book catalogue advertises R. P. Nelson's *Design of Advertising* as "profusely illustrated with examples of good (and bad) ads." The *(and bad)* keeps the main text honest. The main text boasts of good ads. The offstage voice insists the bad ads can't be ignored. And it gives its little wink, suggesting the bad ads are pretty interesting.

The whispered aside can take any tone. It can be flippant:

He promised to come (fat chance).

Or delighted:

He promised to come (yea).

Or considerate:

He promised to come. (But will this disrupt your plans?)

Or cataclysmic:

My very photogenic mother died in a freak accident (picnic, lightning) when I was three.

Or meticulous, hard working, "scholarly":

He was eager for fame ("Fame is the spur that the clear spirit doth raise," he announced) and so wrote a pastoral elegy, a poetic form then much in vogue.

Or merely helpful in a bibliographical way:

Examples apart, I used dashes only once in discussing the dash (third paragraph, first sentence).

George Orwell finished *1984* in 1948, and it was published the next year (London, Secker & Warburg; New York, Harcourt, Brace).

The Colon

The colon does just one thing: it points ahead. It is an arrow on the page ⟶ or, as you sometimes see in old books, a hand like this ☞ insisting, "hey, look here."

He found what he had been looking for: hard work, low pay, and ignominy.

My message is simple enough: write as you talk.

A colon introduces words, phrases, and sentences. It is always introducing, and what it introduces, the stuff on its far side, is always more important than what comes before it. In *Let Us Now Praise Famous Men,* a book about Southern sharecroppers in the 1930s, James Agee occasionally wrote a colon and left blank two lines below it. By this odd device he wanted readers to understand that nothing he could say about the sharecroppers' plight had any standing alongside the terrible *fact* of it. The fact of it was literally unspeakable. All Agee could do was try to make us, his readers, as open to it as he was: lead us toward it: coax us: point:

If we had eyes we would see what he wanted us to.[3]

[3] I am here borrowing an idea from myself. See my *Documentary Expression and Thirties America,* New York and London, 1973, p. 311.

As you know, reader, this is a numbered footnote. Unlike an *asterisked* footnote, which must be put at the bottom of the page where its reference is (see for example

The Semicolon

If my students are a fair sample, the semicolon is the hardest punctuation mark to master; it is certainly the least important.

The thing to remember about the semicolon is that you never have to use it. You can always replace it with something else just as correct. This is because the semicolon, as we now understand it, is itself a substitute for other punctuation marks, namely the comma and the period.

Used correctly, the semicolon is either a heavy comma (1) or, much more often, a light period (2).

1. As a heavy comma, the semicolon occurs in complicated sentences like the following from Bruno Bettelheim's *The Uses of Enchantment:*

To enrich [a child's] life, [a story] must stimulate his imagination; help him to develop his intellect and to clarify his emotions, be attuned to his anxieties and aspirations; give full recognition to his difficulties, while at the same time suggesting solutions to the problems which perturb him.

I said the sentence was complicated, but it's really not. It's just *long.* Essentially it's a list: "To enrich a child's life, a story must 1, 2, 3, 4." Since 1, 2, 3, 4 are phrases in a series, according to our comma rule 7 (page 155) they should be separated by commas. Why aren't they? Well, they *could* have been. Semicolons are never necessary. In place of the three semicolons Bettelheim used in this sentence he could have

---

page 27), a numbered footnote may go there or at the end of the chapter or—as is most common these days (because cheapest)—at the end of the paper, article, thesis, monograph, dissertation, or book. My *Documentary Expression and Thirties America* follows a recent practice and uses both numbered and asterisked footnotes. The numbered footnotes, which give bibliographical information, are grouped at the back of the book. The asterisked footnotes, which give information throwing sidelights on the main text, go on the page where their reference is. On one page, 264, I have *three* such footnotes: *, **, and ***. Three is one or two too many but the information seemed to me too peripheral to squeeze into the main text and yet too good to leave out or bury in the notes at the back of the book.

used three commas (". . . stimulate his imagination, help him to develop his intellect and to clarify his emotions, be attuned to his anxieties and aspirations, give full recognition . . ."). The reason he put semicolons instead of commas was that the last phrase—". . . give full recognition to his difficulties, while at the same time suggesting solutions . . ."—already has a comma in it, and if Bettelheim had used commas to set off the 1, 2, 3, 4 phrases, the reader would have briefly thought that the comma after "difficulties" introduced phrase 5.

No great problem, you say. No, but the sort of problem the semicolon-as-heavy comma avoids. And we can now make clearer when such semicolons are used. *If a sentence has commas separating items in a series and has other commas too—or has colons or dashes—then semicolons may be substituted for the commas separating the items in a series.* Example: a student on H. Rider Haggard's *She*:

Haggard adds to the impact of his adventure by putting it in the form of a memoir; by writing errors into it so that he, as editor, can correct them in footnotes; and by introducing a mass of meticulous details in describing far-away places, the people who inhabit them and their customs.

Example: the anthropologist Edmund Carpenter in *Oh, What a Blow that Phantom Gave Me*:

Nearly the whole of Western culture was organized around one sense: the eye; expressed in one medium: language; and structured according to one model: the book.

Reader, you understand that the semicolons in these examples could as well be commas. Most English-language writers live their allotted span without ever using a semicolon in place of a comma-in-a-series. You should recognize that the semicolon-as-heavy-comma exists, but you never need employ it.

2. The other correct way of using the semicolon is as a light period. Henry Thoreau in *Walden*:

I had more visitors while I lived in the woods than at any other period of my life; I mean that I had some.

As a light period, the semicolon joins independent sentences which so closely interact that to separate them by a period would reduce the flow of meaning between them. Of course Thoreau could have punctuated the sentences

I had more visitors while I lived in the woods than at any other period of my life. I mean that I had some.

But to do so would reduce the punch of his joke.

Or consider a simpler case. Paul Copperman, *The Literacy Hoax:*

Many traditional and rigorous courses have been replaced with fare best described as educational entertainment. Courses in film literature and science fiction are replacing English composition; courses in contemporary world issues and comparative revolutions are replacing world history.

Here the semicolon is used to show the equivalence—temporal, logical, moral—of the two sentences beginning "courses in . . ." The introductory sentence—"Many traditional and rigorous courses have been replaced . . ."—states a thesis that is demonstrated by evidence brought forward in the second and third sentences. These sentences are interchangeable —the third could as well be second—and the semicolon between them helps signal this. What would be lost if a period replaced this semicolon? Nothing much: a nuance perhaps.

You see what the semicolon-as-light-period does: it joins independent sentences and, so doing, calls attention to their *interdependence,* their relationship. It is a subtle punctuation mark, and I am interested to notice who uses it nowadays and who doesn't. Reporters and popular writers seldom use it. They seem to feel it's stuffy and would slow their readers down. Serious writers use it, particularly when they want to emphasize just how serious they are. However, some writers of high aspiration—Ernest Hemingway may have been the first—go out of their way to avoid it. College students use it, probably for the reason popular writers don't: it feels "academic."

The semicolon is one thing you can do without. If you have trouble using it, don't.

The Apostrophe

The apostrophe is an unnecessary punctuation mark used in contradictory ways. No wonder it's used so badly.

Let's give it another try.

Rule 1. Use an apostrophe to show where you've omitted letters when contracting a word:

you've	let's	it's	couldn't
ma'am	nat'l	fo'c'sle	o'er
h'lo	goin'	'cause	'sides

NOTE: *It's* is the contraction of *it is* ("No wonder it's used so badly"). It is also the contraction of *it has* ("It's been good to know you").

Rule 2.

a. Use an apostrophe plus *s* when you want to indicate possession:

Tom's friend	an idea of Hegel's
a worker's rights	an hour's temptation
the children's teachers	another's opinion
her sister-in-law's lawyer's advice	

NOTE: *Dagmar and Jeff's parents* (or *hairdresser*) means Dagmar and Jeff share the same parents (or hairdresser). *Dagmar's and Jeff's parents* (or *hairdresser*) means they have different parents (or hairdressers).

b. When a word ends in *s*, simply add an apostrophe to indicate possession:

the rabbits' cage	the witness' answer[4]
James' book[4]	the Joneses' house
others' work	Arkansas' governor[4]

---

[4] Because I have made this rule simpler than many usage authorities make it, some of them would disagree with my punctuation here. E. B. White would write *James's*

EXCEPTION: The word *its* is the possessive of *it*. It doesn't take an apostrophe: *The dog found its bone.*

THEREFORE: The word *it's* means *it is* or *it has*. The word *its* means possession. The word *its'* doesn't exist.

Rule 3. Use an apostrophe plus *s* when you want to make letters or Arabic numbers plural:

> Dot your i's, cross your t's, mind your p's and q's.
> the 1930's   B-52's   figure 8's
> GI's   V.I.P.'s   IOU's   bb's

NOTE: This apostrophe is used *very* seldom. It is used with letters and Arabic numbers *only*. It should not be used with other plural nouns. The apostrophes in the following sentences are wrong:

Cheerleaders and Kick Team's copying the Rangerette type wriggled and jiggled for the masculine benefit.

I was so nervous my knee's were shaking.

Bachelor's and bachelor girl's are a special breed.

I try to avoid this apostrophe. I don't use it when two or more letters or numbers are used together. Thus I write *GIs* not *GI's*, *V.I.P.s* not *V.I.P.'s*, *1930s* not *1930's*, *B-52s* not *B-52's*. I use the apostrophe only when there is just one letter or number: *Their papers got the C's they deserved.*

The Hyphen

The hyphen is used

1. At the end of a line where, for reasons of space, a word is split between syllables and con-

---

book but also *Moses' book*. The Associated Press would write *James' book* but also *the witness's answer* (and yet, astonishingly, *the witness' story*). United Press International would write *the witness's story* but also *Tennessee Williams' play*. The New York *Times* would write *Arkansas's governor* but also *Kansas' governor*. All these authorities have reasons for their quirks of punctuation, but the reasons are hairsplitting and hard to remember. Use my rule, and if editors want to add an extra *s* after your apostrophes, assume they know why they are doing it.

tinued on the next line, as *continued* just was. Some writers try
to break one-syllable words—like *threw* or *through*—to make
them fit the end of a line. This is not possible in English. A
one-syllable word can't be hypenated and so can't be broken
at the end of a line. A dictionary gives a word's syllabication
(as, SYL-LAB-I-CA-TION), which shows where the word can be
hyphenated.

2. To show a word's syllabication (as you just saw).

3. To spell out something letter by letter: *e-r-s-a-t-z, Z-a-i-r-
e-a-n.*

4. Between compound numbers from twenty-one through
ninety-nine when they are written out: *forty-two, three hundred
seventy-sixth platoon.*

5. To denote a range of numbers: *pp. 23-38, 1939-45.*

6. As an indication of hesitant speech or stuttering: "The
m-m-monster? W-what monster?"

7. Where a common element is omitted from one of a pair
of words: *wind-, rain-, or hailstorm; superwomen and -men.*

On this much, educated writers of English agree. There is a
good deal less agreement on the hyphen's use between compound words. To write *middle-class hang-up* is correct, but so is
middle class hang-up and, some would say, *middleclass hang up*
(or *hangup).* There are writers who hyphenate most compound words. There are writers who hyphenate few. A Journalism teacher at my university tells students not to hyphenate compound words because it is the syntax that makes them
compound, not a punctuation mark. The phrase *the Army-
Navy game* needs no hyphen, he would say, because no one
would read *the Army Navy game* as anything but a game between Army and Navy. Similarly *an all but deserted field* is as
clear as, and emptier than, *an all-but-deserted field.*

Because there is disagreement about the hyphen between
compound words and because few people care whether this
hyphen is used or abused, you can use it as you like, without
middle class hang-ups, and probably not be punished. But for
your information, here is the way I hyphenate—and don't
hyphenate—compound words.

1. If the compound words are used as a noun, I look in the dictionary to see if they are hyphenated or written as one or two words (I had to look up *hang-up*). Dictionaries are always behind the times—Webster's still says "coworker" should be written "co-worker"—and I sometimes don't follow their advice. Nonetheless, it's nice to know whom you are disobeying. If the words aren't in the dictionary (as, *apartment hunting, art-joking-at-art*), I don't have the fun of disobedience.

2. When I use compound words as adjectives, I don't hyphenate them if they follow the noun they modify. Thus,

a baby-blue leisure suit but *a leisure suit of baby blue*

ship-to-shore communication but *communication ship to shore.*

I try not to hyphenate if a compound-word adjective is, like *middle class,* used all the time as an unhyphenated noun. Thus, I write *high school senior* rather than *high-school senior.*

3. I don't hyphenate verbs, unless the dictionary tells me to ("WHITELAW SOFT-PEDALS ON RIOT MEASURES"— headline in *The Guardian*) or the two words say the same thing *(she tut-tutted at my mistake; the pail bang-clattered down the stairs)*. A student wrote (see page 126), "I am often not sure where to cut-off one sentence and begin another"—in which sentence the hyphen is wrong.

4. Otherwise, I generally use a hyphen. Thus

the proverbial ten-foot pole

bone-shaking bounces

one-syllable, four-letter, Anglo-Saxon words

Dwight Macdonald's all-of-a-topic-in-one-place rule

a test-tube-baby clinic [a *test-tube baby clinic* would be a clinic for infant test tubes].

The Ellipsis

An ellipsis indicates that a word or words are omitted from a quote.

A three-dot ellipsis (. . .) shows that what is omitted begins *within* a sentence. A four-dot ellipsis (. . . .) shows that what is omitted begins immediately *after* a sentence, the extra dot being the period from that sentence. With either sort of ellipsis the amount omitted may be as short as a word or as long as several sentences. In the quote on page 72

> Any idea, any book can . . . be suggested in a sentence or expounded in twenty volumes

we are given nearly all of C. Wright Mills' sentence, with just a word or two left out. In the quote on page 95

> The reader of these pages should not look for detailed documentation of every word. . . . To fill in the gaps in my knowledge was out of the question. I had to write now or not at all. And I wanted to write

we lose at least the start of one of Johan Huizinga's sentences, and perhaps *all* that sentence and indeed sentences following.

Be sparing with ellipses (plural of *ellipsis*). Used abundantly they make a passage look like it has acne and sound like a telegram. Further, they may make readers feel that something is being hidden from them.

Even when I begin quoting after the first word of a sentence, I don't put an ellipsis at the start of the quote if the quote makes sense by itself. Thus, though the American patriot Patrick Henry actually said, "I know not what course others may take; but as for me, give me liberty, or give me death!" I would quote his crucial words as "Give me liberty, or give me death!" not ". . . give me liberty, or give me death!" or ". . . [G]ive me liberty, or give me death!"

The ellipsis has one other use. It indicates that a speaker or writer is . . . temporarily at a loss.

Editorial Interruptions

I have just come across a quote I want you to read. It's from an essay by George Orwell:

One's first feeling is that in describing Shakespeare as a bad writer he [novelist Leo Tolstoy] is saying something demonstrably untrue. But this is not the case. In reality there is no kind of evidence or argument by which one can show that Shakespeare, or any other writer, is "good."[5]

Okay. I ask you now to ignore what Orwell said, though, as you know, I agree with it, and look at the words "novelist Leo Tolstoy." These words are mine. They are an editorial interruption (or editorial interpolation) in quoted matter and as such are set off by brackets: [ ].

You use brackets when you interrupt a quote with a clarifying word or phrase of your own. The word or phrase may be in addition to the quoted words, as my "novelist Leo Tolstoy" was, or they may replace the word or words they explain:

One's first feeling is that in describing Shakespeare as a bad writer [Leo Tolstoy, author of *War and Peace* and *Anna Karenina*] is saying something demonstrably untrue.

There are three points to be made about brackets, the first two of them unimportant.

1. Newspapers don't use brackets. They use parentheses instead. There are historical reasons for this, the chief of which is that

2. the standard typewriter doesn't have brackets. When the typewriter was invented late in the last century, people didn't appreciate the importance of brackets and left them off the keyboard in favor of things like %, #, +, =, 1/4, 1/2, and @. When you type on a machine without brackets, don't try to construct them out of what you're given (as, */*) because such

---

[5] "Lear, Tolstoy and the Fool," in *The Collected Essays, Journalism and Letters of George Orwell*, IV:290.

leaning boxes require too much of your time to build and too much of the reader's time to figure out. Instead, make the brackets with pen or pencil.

3. Use brackets as seldom as you can. Like quotations they demand extra energy of the reader. If used too much—used, that is, when a quote is fully comprehensible without them— they make the writer seem a busybody. This is particularly true, I think, of the brackets most frequently used, the "[sic]," which tells the reader that a mistake is in the original quotation *(sic* is a Latin word meaning *thus)* and not in the writer's transcription of it.

We have become a generation of children who have acquired a loosning [sic] grasp on the english [sic] language.

That's a sentence I quote on page 124, but I quote it there without adding the *sics.* There are other errors I have quoted without comment. Here are three. Note what happens when I do comment:

When I try to lengthen a paper, the meaning is sometimes lost or dilluted [sic], and the paper becomes awkward.

Vocabulary fascinates me and I love to exercise it whenever possible. A mistake along the same line of my basic problem; [sic] simplicity.

The forms of entertainment subconsciously effect [sic] one more than other influences in today's world.

Far from being impressed with the chap who put in the *sics,* I think we loathe him. How self-satisfied he seems. What a know-it-all.

Unless you are engaged in the demeaning, if sometimes necessary, sort of criticism that points out another writer's stupidity, I advise you to go light on the *sics.* If there's a trivial mistake in a quote you're using—a misspelling, say— either silently correct it or silently leave it as it is. (Another option: if you're footnoting the quote, make the correction and say that you did so in the footnote.)

Sic is an editorial interpolation you can probably do without, as I do throughout this book. Brackets, on the other hand, are indispensible. When quoting someone, you have a triple responsibility: to yourself and what you are saying (of course), to your reader (if you agree with me), and to the person quoted. Often the best way to meet these responsibilities is to insert bracketed words that help translate the quoted person's meaning into the context of your argument. Trying to do this, I have used dozens of brackets in this book, including two pairs in one of E. D. Hirsch, Jr.'s sentences:

In order to avoid giving the false impression that there is anything permanent about an interpretative validation [which is to say, a "proof"] or the consensus [of belief] it aims to achieve, I now prefer the term "validation" to the more definitive-sounding word "verification."

Punctuating Sentences with Quotes in Them

My students have difficulty punctuating sentences with quoted words in them, and there is good reason why they do. We Americans punctuate such sentences in ways both inconsistent and illogical.

We write:

1. The word everyone used to describe the food was "revolting."
2. Ann tasted the food and said, "Revolting!"
3. Ben called the food "revolting!" and threw his plate on the floor.
4. "The food," said Peg, "is revolting."
5. Sam said the food was "revolting" and then ate it all.
6. Sam said the food was "revolting," and then he ate it all.
7. Flo had to admit it, "The word to describe this food is 'revolting.'"
8. "The food is revolting," said Tad. "Let's talk about something else."

These sentences suggest that if there is punctuation at the end of a quote the punctuation comes *before* the final quote mark. True so far, but not always true:

9. Did Ann really say the food was "revolting"?
10. "Did Ann say the food was 'revolting'?" Bob asked.

11. How nervy to call the food "revolting"!
12. Dot called the food "revolting"—which doesn't mean it wasn't.
13. Tim said the food was "revolting": pasty and bland and full of hairs.
14. Pat called the food "revolting"; she also complained that the water was greasy.

Sentences 1 through 14 are punctuated correctly by American standards. If you are writing for an American audience, you should punctuate sentences with quoted words in them as I have punctuated these.

Though nine of the sentences are punctuated as British writers would punctuate them, five are not. The five suggest the main difference between American and British punctuation:

CORRECT AMERICAN PUNCTUATION	CORRECT BRITISH PUNCTUATION
The word everyone used to describe the food was "revolting."	The word everyone used to describe the food was "revolting".
"The food," said Peg, "is revolting."	"The food", said Peg, "is revolting."
Sam said the food was "revolting," and then he ate it all.	Sam said the food was "revolting", and then he ate it all.
Flo had to admit it, "The word to describe this food is 'revolting.'"	Flo had to admit it, "The word to describe this food is 'revolting'."
"The food is revolting," said Tad. "Let's talk about something else."	"The food is revolting", said Tad. "Let's talk about something else."

As you see, the British way of punctuating sentences with quoted words in them is more logical than the American. The British do not punctuate before the final quotation mark unless the punctuation is part of the quote. The British argue that *"The food", said Peg, "is revolting"* makes more sense than *"The food," said Peg, "is revolting"* because when Peg spoke the original sentence ("The food is revolting") it had no comma after *food.*

All of us realize that there are slight differences between American and British English. The British spell *realize* r-e-a-l-i-s-e, *labor* l-a-b-o-u-r, and *defense* d-e-f-e-n-c-e. They call quotation marks *inverted commas,* periods *full stops,* zeros *naughts,* and French fries *chips.* They understand 1/11/74 as November 1, 1974, rather than January 11, 1974. Such differences are trivial.

As are the differences in the way we punctuate quoted words. Americans read books printed in Britain without any difficulty and vice versa. One system of punctuation is automatically exchanged for the other when something is printed in both the U.K. and the U.S. (a Britisher would have written "the UK and the US"). Thus the Englishman George Orwell wrote,

There is no kind of evidence or argument by which one can show that Shakespeare, or any other writer, is "good".

But I, an American, quoted him as having written,

There is no kind of evidence or argument by which one can show that Shakespeare, or any other writer, is "good."

Many American students today are learning the British system of punctuating quoted words—I don't know how or why. And some American celebrities prefer the British system in their press releases. After his 1978 reelection campaign, U.S. Senator John Tower sent a letter to the Philip Morris Political Action Committee thanking it for a contribution. The letter included this sentence:

As you know, my races can never be considered "easy".

It's reasonable that the period go outside the quotation mark, and it would be correct were Tower a Yorkshireman *standing* for Parliament instead of a Texan *running* for the Senate. Things being as they are, though, Tower's punctuation is incorrect and un-American ("unAmerican," the British would say).

Keep your punctuation inside the quote when it's the American custom to do so. The custom is illogical but it's ours.

Parallel Construction (Abbreviation: || Cons)

Parallel construction—or "parallelism," as it is sometimes and more vaguely called—is the grammatical requirement that similar parts of speech be put in similar places in one sentence or, occasionally, adjacent sentences.

Tommy swam and fished in the lake and hunting in the forest.

Parallel construction is important because faults in parallel construction, like the word *hunting* in the example above, are so conspicuous. Such faults show that their author doesn't have a command of English even when it's logical and, by that fact, simple. Since English is often neither logical nor simple (which is, of course, part of its charm), writers who have trouble with parallel construction are in trouble a good deal of the time.

Look at the example again: "Tommy swam and fished in the lake and hunting in the forest." *Swam* and *fished* are words in parallel, separated by *and*. They are verbs that show what the subject, *Tommy*, did. *Hunting*, a word parallel to them, also separated by the word *and*, means to be the same kind of word. But it isn't. Its *ing* ending tells you that it's not a verb: educated speakers don't say, "Tommy hunting." The participle "hunting" must be made *correctly* parallel, must be changed to a verb. "Tommy swam and fished in the lake and hunted in the forest." Or: "Tommy swam and fished in the lake and went hunting in the forest."

Parallel construction makes only one demand of writers: that they be consistent. It says, "If you treat Peter this way, treat Paul also." A student discusses the film *Hair:*

The isolation of Berger in this episode allows the audience to be put in his place and feel the alarmed paranoia of walking onto a giant cargo plane, landing in a strange place, and only to commit body and soul to a war that he disagrees with.

The student was going along fine, setting up parallel participial phrases—". . . *walking* onto a giant cargo plane, *landing* in a strange place . . ."—when for no apparent reason he used an infinitive—". . . to commit . . ."—in place of a participle and thus broke parallel construction. He should have kept to the form he started with: ". . . walking . . . landing . . . and committing body and soul to a war he hates."

Verbs, participles, and infinitives used in parallel positions must be in the same form. Tennyson's Ulysses grown old is not only heroic but grammatical when he pledges

> To strive, to seek, to find, and not to yield.

Some novice writers apparently think such consistency of form boring. They like to have a variety of verb forms in parallel position. The result is confusion:

There are several possibilities I came up with: returning home to live, work, and attend Odessa Junior College to get some of my basic required courses out of the way; drop out of school here for a semester to earn money to continue later; or to try to continue now while working and accepting a loan.

The verb form that introduces each possibility should be the same: ". . . returning home . . . dropping out . . . trying to continue . . ." or ". . . return home . . . drop out . . . try to continue . . ." or ". . . to return home . . . to drop out . . . to try to continue . . ."

What I've said about infinitives, participles, and verbs applies much more widely. You need to be concerned about parallel construction whenever you have words, phrases, clauses, or sentences in a series of two or more. A student gives her final evaluation of a book:

God's Smuggler tends to challenge the Christian in his appreciation of Scripture, feelings concerning money, and his faith in the power of God.

The phrases at the end of the sentence aren't fully parallel: if *faith* has a *his* before it, so must *feelings*. (As you do unto Peter, so Paul.) Thus you could say ". . . his appreciation . . . his feelings . . . and his faith . . ." or ". . . his appreciation . . . feelings . . . and faith . . ." (Incidentally, notice the timidity of that ". . . tends to challenge . . ." It's your opinion—be bold: *"God's Smuggler* challenges the Christian . . .")

A freshman writes about her life as an athlete at the university where I teach:

Materially you receive many fringe benefits such as: traveling, meeting new people, special treatment in getting your classes, and most important, if one is on scholarship, they get a free ride through school.

As often happens, it is the last straw in the series that breaks parallel construction. We are given "traveling [noun], meeting [participle used as a noun] new people, special treatment [noun modified by the adjective *special]* in getting your classes, and most important, if one is on scholarship, they get a free ride through school [a whole sentence!]." The student was describing the experience of the abstract *you,* an athlete at the University of Texas at Austin ("Materially you receive . . ."). There was no reason for her to shift abstractions in mid-sentence and start speaking of *one* or *they* (". . . if one is on scholarship, they get . . ."). This is a fault in agreement. But even with this fault corrected the fault in parallel construction remains. Simply, the noun-noun-noun formation must be followed by another noun, not by a sentence. So:

Materially you receive many fringe benefits such as traveling, meeting new people, special consideration in getting your classes when you need them, and most important, if you are on scholarship, a free ride [noun modified by the adjective *free* and the article *a]* through school.

Paired, or "correlative," conjunctions like *either . . . or, neither . . . nor, both . . . and, as . . . as, not only . . . but* (or *but also*) always introduce words in parallel. A student writing about I forget what:

This may neither be a necessity nor advisable.

No. Since *neither* is followed by a verb, *nor* must be too:

This may neither be a necessity nor be advisable.

Or, better sounding but no more correct:

This may be neither necessary nor advisable.

A student writing of boys' and girls' sports:

Inequality in high school basketball exists not only with money but also facilities.

No. *Not only* introduces a preposition, *with*. So must *but also* (note that the preposition doesn't have to be *with*):

Inequality in high school basketball exists not only with money but also in facilities.[6]

A final point. The need for parallel construction sometimes extends beyond an individual sentence to adjacent sentences. A student-hitchhiker:

Most people pick hitchhikers up for two reasons; first they may just want to help you out or they just want company to cut the boredom of their travel.

The latter part of this passage is haunted by the ghost of an unspoken *second* or *next* or *then too*. When you say "first" or "in the first place" or "on the one hand," you must tell us when you give us a "second" or "next place" or "other hand." For example:

There are two reasons why people pick up hitchhikers. First, some people are kind and want to help others. Second, some people want company to cut the boredom of their travel.

---

[6] Even with its parallel construction straight, this is a weak sentence. The way to strengthen it, as so often, is to change its subject to a person-word (see page 100). For example: "Boys playing high school basketball have more money spent on them than girls do."

There are guide words, then, that call for other guide words. This is one form of parallelism between adjacent sentences.

Another form of parallelism we hear in passages like Winston Churchill's "We shall fight on the beaches, we shall fight on the landing grounds . . ." where a writer uses repetition for effect. But repetition isn't only needed in high-flown writing. Our hitchhiker again:

Prior to any lengthy hitching trip I get my hair cut or shape it so it looks short and well groomed. In addition, brightly colored clothes, no blue jeans, with a casual look have worked best.

The sudden *brightly colored clothes* throws us because the first sentence suggested that the "I" was going to give us his experience through himself. Why doesn't he keep the promised parallelism?

For a lengthy hitching trip I get my hair cut short or shape it so it looks short and well groomed. I wear brightly colored casual clothes—not blue jeans, though.

I asked my freshmen to write come-ons for a new magazine of their invention. Here is part of one student's copy:

If you men are tired with having only news and sports magazines to read, get in touch with current trends in *Today's Person*. Likewise, women will receive more benefit from this magazine than women's magazines now on the stands.

Why are the men addressed in such a chummy way—"you men"—and the women treated so coolly, as Third Persons? That won't do.

If you men are tired of news and sports magazines, get in touch with yourself in *Today's Person*. If you women are tired of what "women's" magazines think of you, our magazine, aimed at *Today's* total *Person*, is for you.

Parallel construction is an equal opportunity employer of language: it pledges the same treatment for Peter and Pauline.

We have already said a good deal about footnotes. See for example the footnotes on pages 12 and 27 and the footnote that begins on page 33. Or don't bother: just read on.

There are three kinds of footnotes:

1. Footnotes that amplify or comment on something said in the main text, as the footnote on page 27 does. Let's call this sort of footnote a *commentary* footnote.

2. Footnotes that give bibliographical reference for something said, quoted, or paraphrased in the main text, as the footnote on page 17 does. Let's call this sort of footnote a *bibliographical* footnote.

3. Footnotes that do both 1 and 2. Let's call this sort of footnote *mixed* (the footnote that begins on page 12 is a mixed footnote).

Commentary, bibliographical, and mixed footnotes appear either at the bottom of the page on which they are initiated by something in the main text or *after* the text—that is, at the end of the paper, article, chapter, or book (in which case they are sometimes called "endnotes"). When they appear at the bottom of a page, they are signaled by one or more asterisks (*, **, ***) or other typographical symbols († and # are occasionally used), or they are numbered (1, 2, 3). When they appear at the end of a text, they must be numbered.

The exception. Scientists and social scientists writing for their colleagues use a different method of bibliographical footnoting. They imbed footnotes in the main text, as I did and noted doing on page 30. Imbedded footnotes appear in parentheses either in the sentence that cites what they refer to or at the end of a quote. They look like this:

"If one is a gardener there is something to be said for dying with the dying year" (Betty Massingham, *Miss Jekyll,* London, 1966, p. 170).

Or this:

Historians of English (Baugh and Cable 1978:299) point out that the term *camouflage* was originally used by French stage designers.

Or this:

Chicago defeated St. Louis as preeminent city of the Midwest, Childs says, because it was unhampered by the past (p. 127).

A text using short imbedded footnotes, like those in the last two examples, must be followed by a bibliography giving the complete reference for each work cited. There are several different systems for imbedding footnotes and compiling the bibliography that accompanies them. You should use the form your readers expect. Some single-minded readers (me among them) get annoyed at the way imbedded footnotes interrupt the text with clumps of names and numbers. Annoyance is pointless. The method is standard in scientific and social scientific work. Enough said. End exception.

The kind of footnote most often used is the bibliographical. Indeed when we say a piece of writing is "footnoted," we mean it has bibliographical footnotes. Such footnotes, with the exception of the imbedded variety discussed in the last paragraph, look like this:

1. Gregory Bateson, *Mind and Nature,* New York, 1979, p. 30. [A book.]
2. Roland Barthes, "Writers, Intellectuals, Teachers," in *Image—Music—Text,* ed. and trans. Stephen Heath, n.p. [Great Britain], Fontana, Collins, 1977, p. 194. [Article in a book by the same author, which book is edited (ed.) and translated (trans.) by someone else. The book series (Fontana) and publisher (Collins) are given because the book's title page doesn't mention the city or country where it was published (the n.p. means no place). I knew the book was published in Great Britain and so gave this information in brackets.]
3. Frank Riessman, "The Hidden IQ," in *The New Assault on Equality: IQ and Social Stratification,* eds. Alan Gartner and others, New York, 1974, p. 219. [Article in a book by another author or, here, editors. Alan Gartner is the first editor mentioned on the title page, and the book has more than two editors, or the names of both would be given.]
4. Vincent Crapanzano and Jane Kramer, "A World of Saints and She-Demons," New York *Times Magazine,* June 22, 1969, pp. 14–38. [Article in journal. The volume number isn't necessary if you give the date.]
5. The Royal Shakespeare Company, *Nicholas Nickleby,* adapted from the Dickens

novel by David Edgar, dir. Trevor Nunn and John Caird, Aldwych Theatre, London, June 2, 1981.
[Live performance. Give title, author, director (dir.), producer. Give the location where it occurred, and either the date you saw it or the date it opened.]

6. Woody Allen, dir., *Love and Death,* United Artists, 1975.
[Commercial film. Give title, producer or distributor, year of release, and, usually, director. Give other information—like stars, writer, cinematographer, makeup artist, costume designer—only if such information is relevant to what you are saying.]

7. Pablo Picasso, "The First Steps," oil on canvas, 1943, Yale University Art Gallery, New Haven, Conn.
[Visual art. Give artist, title, medium, year produced, present location or the name of a book or magazine in which the piece is reproduced.]

8. The Captain and Tennille, "Love Will Keep Us Together," by Neil Sedaka and Howard Greenfield, A&M Records, Inc., 1975.
[Pop record. The composer of the song doesn't have to be given.]

9. Igor Stravinsky, *Le Sacre du Printemps* ("The Rite of Spring"), Columbia Symphonia Orchestra conducted by the composer, Columbia Records ML 5719, n.d. [1961?].
[Classical record. Name the principal piece of music, its composer, the orchestra and its conductor, the record company, the record's number (here, ML 5719), and the year the record appeared. The title of the record may be too frivolous to give. No date was given on this record, so I put n.d. and estimated its year of publication in brackets. Rather than "1961?" I could have said "c. 1961" or "ca. 1961" or "circa 1961," all of which mean "about 1961."]

10. Neolithic clay fertility figurine with exaggerated breasts, stomach, and thighs, made in the sixth millennium B.C., found at Çatalhöyük, Turkey, now exhibited in the Museum of Anatolian Civilizations, Ankara. A photo of this figurine is in Raci Temizer, *Museum of Anatolian Civilizations,* English edition, Ankara, Ankara Society for the Promotion of Tourism, Antiquities, and Museums, 1969, p. 7 (lower picture).
[Something by an unknown maker. Tell what you can of when, where, and of what it was made. Tell where it can now be seen.]

The above list shows simple ways to footnote different sorts of writing, media, and artifacts. My footnotes don't exactly follow the form recommended by the Modern Language Association or any other authority. There is no reason they have to, and no reason you should follow what I have done. If you want to, you can make up your own way of bibliographical footnoting so long as (1) you are fairly consistent within each manuscript and (2) you give the name of the artifact you are citing, the name of the person who made it, and date and place it was made, published, exhibited, or seen by you.

After you have cited a piece of writing once, abbreviate subsequent footnotes referring to it. Thus:

1. Barthes, p. 197.
2. Baugh and Cable, p. 35.

When you have footnotes that refer to something you cited many pages ago or when you have footnoted two works by the same person, give the title of what you are quoting as well as the author. Thus:

1. Mills, *The Sociological Imagination,* p. 118.
2. Orwell, "Politics and the English Language," pp. 128–29.

By using this method of subsequent footnoting you can avoid such nuisances as the Latin expressions ibid. (which means "in the same place"), op. cit. ("in the work cited"), and loc. cit. ("in the place cited").

Now the sixty-four-dollar question: when do you *have* to footnote things you cite?

The short answer is: when you want to. The long answer is: when your reader expects you to. The unhappy answer is: when you are told to. You may have noticed that I haven't footnoted much. I quoted Ernest Hemingway and Theodore Dreiser on page 133, for example, and didn't mention where their words came from. I could have,[7] but I thought this information too peripheral to the point I was making for me to clutter the page with it.

Bibliography

A bibliography is a list of things on a certain topic, usually arranged alphabetically by the makers' last names and in a format like the following:

AESCHYLUS, *Seven against Thebes,* trans. David Grene, in *The Complete Greek Tragedies,* eds. Grene and Richmond Lattimore, Chicago, University of Chicago Press, 1959, I:263–304.

[7] Hemingway, "In Another Country," in *The Short Stories of Ernest Hemingway,* New York, 1938, p. 267. Dreiser, *An American Tragedy,* New York, 1925, vol. II, book III, chap. 29, p. 352.

BADHAM, JOHN, dir., *Saturday Night Fever,* with John Travolta, prod. Robert Stigwood, 1977.

BAUGH, ALBERT C., and THOMAS CABLE, *A History of the English Language,* 3d ed., Englewood Cliffs, N.J., Prentice-Hall, Inc. 1978.

DYLAN, BOB, "Mr. Tambourine Man," copyright M. Witlock and Sons, 1964.

Mork and Mindy, with Robin Williams, Henderson Production Co., Inc., and Miller-Milkis Productions, Inc., in association with Paramount Television, first broadcast September 14, 1978, ABC.

YEATS, W. B., "The Fisherman," from *The Wild Swans at Coole,* reprinted in *The Variorum Edition of the Poems of W. B. Yeats,* eds. Peter Ellt and Russell K. Alspach, New York, Macmillan, 1957, pp. 347–48.

I seldom read bibliographies: the naked names don't tell me enough. I do read, and with relish, *annotated* bibliographies, which discuss and evaluate what they name. Annotated bibliographies (or bibliographical essays: the two phrases mean the same thing) aren't alphabetical and take any format their writer likes. They are in fact compendiums of likes and dislikes, roses and brickbats.

Here is a short annotated bibliography on aids to writing.

There are many books that tell you how to improve your writing's form—make it correct and smooth. There are not many books that tell you how to improve your writing's content—make it useful and inventive. (This book has tried to do both things.)

Among the books that teach how to write correctly and smoothly there are three classics. William Strunk, Jr., and E. B. White, *The Elements of Style* (3d ed., New York, 1979) is the best of them. Strunk wrote it in about 1915, and White, who was Strunk's student at Cornell in 1919, rewrote it in about 1958. *The Elements of Style* is great fun to read, but I have found it isn't much help to insecure writers. It is too short (85 pages) to analyze writing problems in detail. Further, it is so clever, so "style" conscious, as to imply that what counts is manner, not content.

The second classic I never finished reading. H. W. Fowler's *Dictionary of Modern English Usage* (1st ed., 1926; 2d ed., revised by Sir Ernest Gowers, 1965; Oxford, London, New York) is a ragbag of long and short articles on words, grammar, syntax, spelling, punctuation, and typography. The book's problem is that it is impossible to know where to find anything in it. J. Arthur Greenwood, *Finding It in Fowler: An Alphabetized Index to the Second Edition (1965) of H. W. Fowler's "Modern English Usage"* (Princeton, 1969) doesn't help because it doesn't index concepts, only important words. Some writers find Fowler a joy to browse in. I don't, but that is certainly the way to read him: aimlessly.

The third classic is Ernest Gowers' *The Complete Plain Words* (London, 1954; Baltimore, 1962), a compilation of his *Plain Words* (1948) and *The ABC of Plain Words* (1951). Gowers is not only more orderly than Fowler, his book has a purpose—"to help officials in their use of written English as a tool of their trade"—and often pays attention to it. Like Fowler, though, Gowers does too many little essays about the use of words few of us want to use ("desiderate," "envisage," "factitious") and wastes time inventing problems no one heard of before *(the abstract appendage, the throw-back comma)* and repairing perfectly good sentences (he would change "World population is increasing faster than world food production" to "The population of the world is increasing faster than the food it produces"). Whereas Fowler's tone is abrasive, Gowers' is good humored.

Sir Arthur Quiller-Couch's *On the Art of Writing* (New York, 1916), a book once thought a classic, is now chiefly interesting as evidence of how much English has changed in this century. Quiller-Couch calls his book "informal" because it was first delivered as a series of lectures at Cambridge University in 1913. Here is an informal sentence of seventy years ago:

You all know that a great part of Lessing's argument in his *Laokoon*, on the essentials of Literature as opposed to Pictorial Art of Sculpture, depends on this—that in Pictorial Art or in Sculpture the eye sees, the mind apprehends, the whole in a moment of time, with the correspondent disadvantage that this moment of time is fixed and stationary; whereas in writing, whether in prose or in verse, we can only produce our effect by a series of successive small impressions, dripping our meaning (so to speak) into the reader's mind—with the correspondent advantage, in point of vivacity, that our picture keeps moving all the while.

One sentence like that is fun. A book of such sentences isn't.

Rudolf Flesch has written half a dozen how-to-write books. None is a classic, perhaps because they are all so much *one* book. Flesch's *How to Write, Speak, and Think More Effectively* (New York, 1960), for example, announces that it "includes material from *The Art of Plain Talk, The Art of Readable Writing, The Art of Clear Thinking, How to Test Readability,* and *A New Way to Better English.*" Flesch's fight against pretentious writing has influenced thousands of people. If your writing is clogged with big words, don't do as I did and wait for middle age to straighten you out. Try Flesch. Don't believe him, though, that "readable" writing can be quantified by counting words per sentence and italics and upper case letters. No: readable writing is writing that says things worth reading. And don't think simple writing has to have the golly-whiz tone Flesch sometimes affects. Such a tone is patronizing, though he means it to be just the opposite.

If you have questions about "correct"—that is, standard— English usage and want to know, say, when to use *lay,* when *lie,* when *as,* when *like,* what a dangling participle is and why and how to avoid it, there are many handbooks to set you straight. Here are four: Roy H. Copperud, *American Usage and Style: The Consensus* (New York, 1979); Bergen and Cornelia Evans, *A Dictionary of Contemporary American Usage* (New York, 1957); Rudolf Flesch, *The ABC of Style: A Guide to Plain English* (New York, 1964); William and Mary Morris, *Harper Dictionary of Contemporary Usage* (New York, 1975).

To help you prepare a text for submission to a teacher or editor, you may need another sort of correctness book. Such books explain typing format, pagination, abbreviation, capitalization, indexes, captions, use of foreign names, and, in great detail, documentation (which means footnotes and bibliography), italicizing, punctuation, and the like. Books of this sort are called, confusingly, style books or style sheets. They are prepared by publishers, periodicals, learned societies, the wire services, and radio and TV stations for the use of their organizations. A few of these style books have been published for the general public's use. The best known of them are the University of Chicago Press, *The Chicago Manual of Style* (13th ed., Chicago, 1982), an earlier edition of which is handily abridged in Kate Turabian, *A Manual for Writers of Term Papers, Theses, and Dissertations* (4th ed., paperback, Chicago, 1973), and the Modern Language Association's *MLA Handbook for Writers of Research Papers, Theses, and Dissertations* (New York, 1977).

So much for books that tell you how to write correctly. As I've said, there are few books that tell you how to write good stuff. This is because the question of what worthwhile writing is seems so rudimentary that novice writers don't dare ask it and experienced writers don't bother answering it. I've known only two people to go out of their way to answer it. One is my colleague Bill Goetzmann, who has been known to ask students writing on a rarefied topic, "What do you know when you know that?" Goetzmann taught me there is magic in the words "so what?" The other is Benjamin De-Mott, an English teacher and frequent magazine contributor. I'm sure that some of my ideas in Chapter 2 are versions of things I heard DeMott say fifteen years ago. DeMott himself has apparently not written on the topic. The closest he comes is in a prickly essay, "Reading, Writing, Reality, Unreality . . ." in his *Supergrow: Essays and Reports on Imagination in America* (New York, 1969, pp. 138–55).

Jessica Mitford's introduction and interchapter notes to *Poison Penmanship: The Gentle Art of Muckraking* (New York, 1979; British title: *The Making of a Muckraker*, London, 1979) offer lively insight into the way a reporter thinks while getting and writing articles. Though Mitford tells little about how she chooses a subject, she lets us see that passion has everything to do with it. For would-be writers, her most interesting article is on the Famous Writers School of Westport, Connecticut. Her description of the school's unscrupulous methods nearly drove it into bankruptcy. The Famous Writers School tries to teach its students to write correctly and colorfully about nothing and holds out the promise that if they do they will be published. "They constantly encourage their students toward a belief in a market that doesn't exist," one former student told Mitford. Said another, "The school attempts to indoctrinate its students with a universally palatable style . . . Forty years ago the sort of bland writing they encourage might have found a home in the mass circulation family magazines—I doubt it would today." Smooth writing doesn't count: useful writing does. Mitford's article, "Let Us Now Appraise Famous Writers," appeared originally in *The Atlantic* (July 1970, pp. 45–54). *Poison Penmanship* reprints the whole thing except for the paragraph in which the second former student says what I quote above.

Among the essential books George Orwell (1903–50) died before writing was one on how to write. Why his work is so convincing I don't know. There must be technical reasons having to do with tone and diction and their relation to the subject. When I read him, though, I don't notice such things. What I know is an honest man is talking to me about something that matters enormously. Orwell left writers a short list of rules, the first of which I disagreed with earlier:

  i.   Never use a metaphor, simile or other figure of speech which you are used to seeing in print.
  ii. Never use a long word where a short one will do.
  iii. If it is possible to cut a word out, always cut it out. [Why not cut the "always"?]
  iv. Never use the passive where you can use the active.
  v.   Never use a foreign phrase, a scientific word or a jargon word if you can think of an everyday English equivalent.
  vi. Break any of these rules sooner than say anything outright barbarous.

This is good, but unremarkable. Orwell's real gift to writers is his writing itself and the lesson it suggests. The lesson is to write about what you really care about and, at some point in your writing, try to explain why you care. Orwell does this all the time—without, however, forcing himself on the reader. A good place to start reading him is *The Road to Wigan Pier* (London, 1937; New York, 1958), his book about poverty among British miners in the 1930s and the class division between those who work with their bodies and those who don't.

Since it is inspiration that counts first and last, maybe the best way to learn to do worthwhile writing is to read some of it. Here are some worthwhile general interest nonfiction books. Mark Twain, *Life on the Mississippi* (1883). Henry Adams, *Mont-Saint-Michel and Chartres* (1904). William Carlos Williams, *In the American Grain* (1925). Ernest Hemingway, *Death in the Afternoon* (1932). James Agee and Walker Evans, *Let Us Now Praise Famous Men* (1941; 2d ed., 1960). James Thomas Flexner, *First Flowers of Our Wilderness: The Colonial Period* (1947; 2d ed. as vol. I of his *History of American Painting*, 1969). Vladimir Nabokov, *Speak, Memory* (original title: *Conclusive Evidence*, 1951). Whittaker Chambers, *Witness* (1952). Robert L. Heilbroner, *The Worldly Philosophers* (1953; 5th ed., 1980). Roland Barthes, *Mythologies* (original French edition, 1957; translated into English by Annette Lavers, 1972). Loren Eiseley, *The Immense Journey* (1957). Alan Moorehead, *The White Nile* (1960) and *The Blue Nile* (1962). Theodora Kroeber, *Ishi in Two Worlds: A Biography of the Last Wild Indian in North America* (1961). Ralph Ellison, *Shadow and Act* (1964). Malcolm X and Alex Haley, *The Autobiography of Malcolm X* (1965). Tom Wolfe, *The Kandy-Kolored Tangerine-Flake Streamline Baby* (1965) and *The Right Stuff* (1979). Calvin Tomkins, *The Bride and the Bachelors: Five Masters of the American Avant-Garde* (1965; expanded edition, 1968). Joan Didion, *Slouching towards Bethlehem* (1968). James D. Watson, *The Double Helix* (1968). John McPhee, *Levels of the Game* (1969). Studs Terkel, *Hard Times: An Oral History of the Great Depression* (1970). Roger Kahn, *The Boys of*

Summer (1972). Stanley Milgram, *Obedience to Authority* (1974). Kurt Vonnegut's essays and autobiographical writing. Julian Jaynes, *The Origin of Consciousness in the Breakdown of the Bicameral Mind* (1976). Philip P. Hallie, *Lest Innocent Blood Be Shed: The Story of the Village of Le Chambon and How Goodness Happened There* (1979). James Fallows, *National Defense* (1981). Janet Malcolm, *Psychoanalysis: The Impossible Profession* (1981). Susan Allen Toth, *Blooming: A Small-Town Girlhood* (1981). Garry Wills, *The Kennedy Imprisonment* (1982). Russell Baker, *Growing Up* (1982).

Though I like and admire these books, I know some have weaknesses, patches of overwriting, repetition, befuddlement. No matter: their content is so strong, the writer's commitment to it so deep, that such nuisances shrink almost to invisibility. May we all find such themes!

POSTSCRIPT

Prefaces tell you why a book was written, but postscripts can as well. Actually, either can do almost anything; they are the jokers in the deck.

While writing this book I have discovered some of the reasons why I wrote it. I don't know all the reasons, of course, and maybe the reasons I don't know are stronger than those I do. There are strong reasons involved, whether I know them or not. Without strong reasons I wouldn't have gotten so far (page 199) and couldn't have spent so long (four years). Anyway, good and bad, here are the reasons I know:

- A little money.

- A little glory.

- My disagreement with the emphasis on "correctness" in composition teaching.

- Vanity. Some of my ideas I thought up by myself; I was proud enough of them to want them published.

- Laziness. I wanted to get the ideas down on paper so I wouldn't have to tell them to my students. I seldom have class time to go through an explanation of what I think about some aspect of writing. When I try to, I usually forget part of the explanation. In this book my ideas have as much force as I can give them.

- A family debt. My father, a banker, and I used to disagree about writing. This book is to show him I finally learned he is right: it's content and straightforwardness that matter, not artistry.

- Vocational zeal. I wanted to write a tribute to English non-fiction prose, the tool I am supposed to teach people to use. I wanted to demonstrate that I respect it enough to try and understand the way it works. This book, I now realize, is a prosaic love song.

- Altruism. I wanted to help my students who have trouble writing. I wanted to help other insecure writers. I wanted to help you, reader.

Though I learned some of the ideas in this book by myself, I certainly didn't learn them alone. Students, teachers, and friends corroborated the ideas, clarified them, sent me back to the drawing board for better ones. In this paragraph I have the pleasure of saying thank you. To Student X and the students of English 308 who made me realize I had changed my mind about writing. To students in other courses who heard me out and helped me out. To all those, named and unnameable, whose opinions are part of this book. To my colleague Tom Cable, who gave more good counsel than a friend should have been asked for, and other readers generous of their time and opinion: David A. Anderson, Lisa Beyer, Chris Brookeman, Robert Crunden, Meg Gertmenian, W. R. Keast, Jim Lewis, Jeffrey Meikle, Lawrence Walker, and Rik Warch. To Judy D'Mello, Mary Ogilvie, Sharon Lee, and Nancy York. To James Raimes, Alice Fasano, Paul Randall Mize, and Estelle Laurence. To Jane, Molly, and Gordon.

And to friends and teachers who took an interest in my attempts to write when I was young.

"Great is the art of beginning," wrote poet Henry Wadsworth Longfellow, "but greater the art is of ending."

I disagree. A beginning makes or breaks a piece of writing because it reveals what the writing is going to say. An ending, as we saw in Chapter 3, may simply summarize what has gone before and thus close the circle:

Here is such an ending, reader, and my farewell:

In your writing, be strong, defiant, forebearing. Have a point to make and write to it. Dare to say what you want most to say, and say it as plainly as you can. Whether or not you write well, write bravely.

Appendix A
STUDENT X'S PAPER REVISITED

Here is the paper again:

WHAT BOTHERS ME ABOUT WRITING

The chief problem I have with writing is not being able to put down in words exactly what my mind is thinking. It has become such a problem that I get parenoid whenever I have to write a paper. In fact, I don't
5 even enjoy writing anymore, instead, it seems more of a hassle.

I wasn't always like this. I enjoyed writing when I was younger and in high school, but ever since my first semester of Freshman English (which was last semester),
10 I've obtained this terrible feeling towards writing papers. I guess it all came about because of the professor I had and what he had to say about my papers that brought my present situation on. It seemed as though whatever I wrote, he had no positive comments about it
15 and all negative ones. This made me lose confidence in my writing ability and it made me feel like I did not know how to write at all.

So now, whenever I begin writing a paper I do not write what comes to my mind, but instead am first con-
20 cerned with the sentence structure, word choice, organization, content, whether it is coherent, or whatever other rules are involved with English writing. I realize this is important to consider, but it has kept me from writing what and how I feel. I feel as if I have been
25 smothering myself with all of these rules and regulations *before* I write so that I can not write. In fact, I feel like it is not even me who is writing the paper. It is like I have lost my own creativity and originality because of this parenoid feeling.
30 I do not like not being able to enjoy writing, because it is such a good way to express one's self. In fact, this is the first paper in which I have expressed myself in exactly the way I feel. I felt very relaxed because I said what I had to say and did not concern myself with the
35 "rules" of English writing. I thank you very much, professor Stott for allowing us to write this paper, because I can say for myself that it took a load off my mind and maybe I can begin to enjoy writing again.

I have already praised this paper's content. I will now discuss the faults in its form I consider worth mentioning.

First, a generalization. There are, I suggest, three kinds of formal writing faults. (Call them faults, errors, mistakes, problems, boo-boos, what you will.) The most important sort of fault I will call

SENSE FAULTS

A sense fault in a piece of writing is anything that changes or confuses what the writing means to say. A sense fault can be caused by many things including bad logic, punctuation, or word choice.

There is one sense fault in Student X's paper. It is in the first sentence of the third paragraph (lines 18–22) and was caused by bad word choice, which in turn was caused either by the misdefinition of a word or by haste. X wrote:

So now, whenever I begin writing a paper I do not write what comes to my mind, but instead am first concerned with the sentence structure, word choice, organization, content, whether it is coherent, or whatever other rules are involved with English writing.

This is a weak sentence. In a general way we see what X means, but his meaning is not sharply put. In fact, because of the sense fault, his meaning is contradicted by part of the sentence. X means to say this: when he writes a paper now, he thinks first about writing correctly rather than about what he wants to say. X tries, as he should, to give us examples of the sort of things he now thinks about first, but he runs dry: ". . . sentence structure, word choice, organization, content, whether it is coherent, or whatever other rules are involved with English writing."

Let's consider X's examples one by one. *Sentence structure:* that's good because it is external to what X wants to say. *Word choice:* ditto. *Organization:* ditto. *Content:* no, that's the wrong word here. Content isn't external to what X wants to say: it *is* what he wants to say. *Whether it is coherent:* the antecedent of *it* is unclear. If X means the antecedent to be *content*, we wonder how a paper's content, its subject, could in itself fail to be coherent. Of course a subject may not be written about coherently, but I doubt there are inherently incoherent subjects (just as I doubt there are subjects inherently not worth writing on). *Or whatever other rules are involved with English writing:* this is an act of desperation, like the losing team's long passes in the seconds before the final gun. X feels he hasn't given enough examples of the rules that impede his writing, so he plunks down this *or whatever* clause. "Include everything I haven't mentioned," he is telling us. (His tone tells us something he didn't mean to tell us. *Or whatever other rules are involved with English writing:* we hear that he doesn't know what the rules are. We hear that the rules are a nasty mystery to him, always surprising him and causing him grief. This is the way many insecure writers feel about the rules of English.)

It is too bad that X lost control of this sentence because it is the heart of his argument. It is especially too bad that he wrote down "content" because this word makes it look as though he didn't know what he was saying. This is a serious sense fault, and by far the most important fault in the paper.

CONVENTIONAL FAULTS

A conventional fault in a piece of writing is anything that all, or nearly all, educated readers would agree is wrong. If you spell *paranoid* "parenoid," most educated readers of English will say you are wrong, you misspelled the word. They will tell you to look it up in a dictionary.

A misspelling is a conventional fault.

In addition to misspellings, conventional faults include things like

· misdefinition of words

· breaking the basic rules of punctuation

· using incorrect verb forms ("They was surprised when we coming by")

· using incorrect pronoun forms ("Me and her gave it to they")

· using double negatives ("During bankruptcy proceedings the holding company announced that neither its officers nor its affiliates had no money")

· certain violations of parallel construction, which fault we discussed in Chapter 5.

Conventional faults occasionally cause sense faults. I once wrote a magazine article in which the word *literalness* got printed *liberalness* at some cost to my meaning. The editor, Suzanne Mantell, sent an apologetic note: "I'm so sorry about the 'liberalness' slip. It was an outright typo, the most pernicious kind—one that disguises itself as another, plausible word to the unwary. We try very hard to avoid it but it does happen."[1]

---

[1] The article was "Visions of America," *Harper's Magazine*, February 1974, p. 81. It was reprinted as "A Photographer Laureate?" in *Photography Annual 1975*, p. 4,

Most conventional faults, however, don't cause sense faults and thus don't matter much. There are four conventional faults in Student X's paper.

1. In lines 3 and 29, *paranoid* is misspelled.
2. In lines 4–6, X writes:

In fact, I don't even enjoy writing anymore, instead, it seems more of a hassle.

The comma after *anymore* should be a semicolon (". . . enjoy writing anymore; instead, it seems . . .") or a period (". . . enjoy writing anymore. Instead, it seems . . ."). Incidentally the comma after *instead* could be omitted.

3. In line 10 the word *obtained* ("I've obtained this terrible feeling towards writing papers") is misused. Student X wanted to write a grander word than *had,* but *had* was the word to use ("I've had this terrible feeling about writing papers"). As we have noted, the effort to write well by using weighty words to make our writing sound impressive most of the time makes us write worse.

4. In line 35 Student X writes:

I thank you very much, professor Stott for allowing us to . . .

This sentence is carelessly punctuated. It should read: ". . . much, Professor Stott, for . . ." Words of direct address are set off by commas before and after. The "p" in *professor* is capitalized because titles are capitalized when used in direct address ("Please, Sergeant, come fast. He's bleeding") and when followed by a proper name: King Lear, Lord Byron, ex-President Nixon, Miss Jones, Student X.

So much for the conventional faults in X's paper.

TASTE FAULTS

A taste fault in a piece of writing is anything a reader or number of readers disapprove of or think wrong. Taste faults are not, like conventional faults, matters of fact *(paranoid* is

with the error intact. Suzanne Mantell kindly gave me permission to quote from her letter to me.

spelled thus) and matters on which educated English readers overwhelmingly agree (a sentence starts with a capital letter). Taste faults are matters of personal opinion.

Does this mean taste faults are less important than conventional faults? Not always. Many conventional faults—misspellings, mispunctuation, miscapitalizations—are trivial. Many taste faults—overwriting, lazy word choice, repetitiveness—I don't consider trivial.

Taste faults are matters of personal opinion: does this mean anybody's opinion is as good as anybody else's? Most educated people would say no. They would say their opinion on matters of taste should be accepted by those who want to write well. The problem with this answer is that much of the time educated people don't have a common opinion.

They agree on the big questions—in the abstract. They are against jargon and verbosity and ineffective writing. But when it comes to specifics, as often as not they disagree whether a piece of writing is verbose here or there (or nowhere) and, if it is, how much effectiveness it loses thereby (if any).

Further, on many small questions of taste, educated writers of English don't agree even in the abstract. Some say you must not start a sentence with an *and* or *but* or *or.* And others say you may do so whenever you like. Some say you shouldn't end a sentence with a preposition. Others say you should use a preposition anywhere it naturally fits in. Some say you should be careful never to split infinitives. Others can't remember what split infinitives are, and tell you to simply ignore them.

This puts us in a tough spot, reader—you and me and everyone who wants to write better. We can find lots of reliable people to fix the conventional faults in our writing. Any educated person with patience and a blue pencil will help. (I gave you my help against conventional faults in Chapter 5.) But who can we count on to improve our taste faults? Whose taste should we trust?

I don't know that we should trust anybody's taste. Not all the time, in all circumstances. I think we should always be looking for writers to learn from and outgrow. And not only writers: *people,* educated and not. Regarding taste, anybody's opinion is potentially as good as anybody else's, and who knows whose opinion will be crucial to you?

In Chapter 4 I gave you my opinions on how to reduce the taste faults in your writing and thus write in a way I think more effective. I hope you learn a lot from what I say—but I'm glad you won't stop looking for *other* opinions.

Enough. There are three taste faults in X's paper I want to talk about.

1. In lines 11–13, X writes:

I guess it all came about because of the professor I had and what he had to say about my papers that brought my present situation on.

X should have put a period after *papers* and cut the rest of the sentence, which is redundant. How is it redundant? It repeats what has already been said. The word *it* early in the sentence refers to X's unhappy "present situation" ("I guess it all came about . . ."), so the last words in the sentence (". . . that brought my present situation on") just say the same thing again.

People write redundant phrases and sentences because they lack confidence. They have had such bad luck writing they can't believe that simply saying something once is enough to have it understood. But it is. I made this point earlier. I hope I made clear then that a certain amount of redundance isn't bad. Indeed a certain amount of redundancy can be helpful. It is all right for most of a sentence to repeat what has already been said so long as the sentence moves on to say *something* new.

2. In lines 16 and 26 Student X uses *like* as a conjunction in ways many educated people consider wrong. X writes:

It made me feel like I did not know how to write at all.

I feel like it is not even me who is writing the paper. It is like I have lost my own creativity . . .

More ink has been spilled over the use of *like* as a conjunction than over any other fault in English. Sorry to spill more.

Many educated people would say that X's use of *like* is just as wrong as spelling *paranoid* "parenoid." I disagree. (Some educated people would agree with me.) Many educated people would say that X's use of *like* would be improper in formal writing of the sort that appears in books, periodicals, speeches, business correspondence, and ads for Cadillacs. They would substitute other words for *like,* like the following:

It made me feel that [or *as if* or *as though*] I did not know how to write at all.

I feel that [or *as if* or *as though*] it is not even me who is writing the paper. It is as if [or *as though*] I have lost my own creativity.

I agree that X's use of *like* is too casual for most formal writing, but I think it is fine in X's informal paper. Many of us use *like* this way when speaking, and X's paper means to have a speaking tone. Substituting the other words for *like* in X's sentences make the sentences sound pompous—sound, as X says, like someone else wrote them.

The rules for what is "proper" language are agreements among users of the language. Such rules change over time, and when one of them does what the *like* rule does and goes against earlier and everyday usage, economy of words, and common sense, it doesn't stay a rule long. There are signs that the conjunction *like* is becoming acceptable in formal writing. An Associated Press dispatch (May 5, 1980):

The rejuvenated [Jimmy] Connors, playing like he did back in the mid-70s when he was the No. 1 tennis player in the world, destroyed [John] McEnroe in every phase of the match.

To show that's no fluke, an AP dispatch of a year earlier (May 5, 1979) on an antismoking election in Miami:

The tobacco industry, like it did in California last fall, is bankrolling a big-powered campaign to defeat the measure.

The point to make here, I think, is that taste faults shouldn't concern you much. Like Student X and the AP,

you need only write as properly as meets the purpose for
which you are writing.

3. I have already said that line 35—"I thank you very
much, professor Stott for allowing us . . ."—has conventional faults in it. I want to suggest now that it has a more
important taste fault. It is slightly servile. Be careful with
flattery: it is as dangerous as criticism.

Those are the main faults in Student X's paper. They don't
harm the paper much. Certainly the paper is comprehensible
with them. Even with the sense fault: we see through it to
what X means.

Writing faults don't matter much. If your writing has something worthwhile to say, as X's did, most people will overlook its faults. If you have really important things to say,
people will correct the faults for you.

Appendix B
FREE WRITING

I think I was too hard on free writing (see page 44). True, I can't do it myself for more than a few minutes at a time; beyond this, I am overcome by shame and boredom at the dumb things I am saying. But I can free write those few minutes, until my stream of thought runs dry, and I now realize I sometimes do.

What happens is this. I am working on one part of an article, say, concentrating as hard as I can, when, out of the blue, I get an idea of what I might say in another part of the article. Rather than start writing that part and lose what I am concentrating on, I grab a fresh sheet of paper and free write what has crossed my mind: jot it down any which way, using the first words I think of, however awkward or approximate. Later I rework my free writing into a finished paragraph.

I use free writing, then, for a kind of note taking. I have never had a good idea come to me *through* free writing, but I now think this may be a sign of how constrained I am. Sigmund Freud believed that when you free associate—that is, write or say aloud whatever comes to mind, without any restraint—you are led to reveal your inner self. Psychoanalysis, the technique Freud invented, tries to help people understand themselves better by training them to interpret their free associations. Psychoanalysts have found that it takes most people a long while to learn to free associate successfully; some people are never able to do it. I may be one of those people, but I plan to give free writing another try and see whether it enriches what I have to say.

Freud thought free association, unfettered mental play, at the heart of the creative process. In *The Interpretation of Dreams* he quotes a 1788 letter written by the poet Friedrich Schiller to a critic-friend who complained of weak creative powers:

The cause of your complaint lies, it seems to me, in the restraint your intellect imposes on your imagination. I will make my idea more concrete with a simile. Apparently it is not good—indeed it hinders the mind's creative work—if Reason makes too close an examination of ideas as they come pouring in—at the very gateway, as it were. Looked at in isolation, an idea may seem trivial or absurd, but it may be important in relation to another idea that comes after it. Perhaps, in conjunction with other ideas that seem equally absurd, it will form an effective link. Reason cannot judge these ideas unless it retains each one long enough to look at it in connection with the others. When a mind is creative, Reason has withdrawn its watchers from the gates; ideas rush in pell-mell; and only then does Reason look them over. You critics . . . are ashamed or frightened of the momentary excesses that are found in all truly creative minds . . . You complain of having little to write because you reject too soon and discriminate too severely.

I decided to rethink my opinion of free writing when I found that Freud was helped toward this theory of free association by an essay titled "Die Kunst, in drei Tagen ein Originalschriftsteller zu werden" ("The Art of Becoming an Original Writer in Three Days") and then read part of the essay. The essay was written by Ludwig Börne (1786–1837), a German journalist and satirist, in 1823. In about 1870, at age thirteen or fourteen, Freud was given Börne's collected works, which he read avidly. Twenty years later, in the early 1890s, he came up with the technique of free association, apparently influenced by a half-forgotten ("unconscious," he would say) memory of Börne's recipe for creativity. Rereading Börne's essay in 1919, Freud commented: "I was amazed to see how much in it agrees practically word for word with things I have always maintained and thought. He could well have been the real source of my originality."

Börne's essay, though short, seems never to have been published in English translation. I offer it here, slightly retitled, in a translation by my colleague Heide Ziegler and me. Börne's essay is Romantic in its assumptions and somewhat disjointed in its argument. He obviously began it as a joke.

HOW TO BECOME AN ORIGINAL WRITER IN THREE DAYS[1]

There are people and books that claim they can teach Latin, Greek, or French to anyone in three days; they claim to be able to teach accounting in three hours. But nobody has demonstrated how to become an original writer in three days. And yet it is so easy! Nothing need be learned, only much unlearned; nothing need be experienced, only several things forgotten.

The way the world is nowadays the minds of scholars, and thus their books, resemble old palimpsests, from which the boring squabbles of some stepfather of the Church or the gibberish of some monk must first be scraped in order to reveal the Roman classic beneath. Every human mind contains beautiful and—since the world is created anew with every soul born into it—original thoughts. But life and education inscribe their useless facts into the mind and cover up those thoughts. One will get a fairly correct view of these matters if one considers the following. We always recognize animals, fruits, or flowers in their natural forms; they are what they appear to be. But would anyone who knows only partridge pâté, raspberry juice, or attar of rose perceive the true nature of a partridge or a raspberry bush or a rose?

That is the way things stand with the sciences, and with everything else that is grasped through the mind and not through the senses: everything is dressed and changed before being dished out, and we never get to know anything in its raw and naked form. Public opinion is the kitchen where every truth is butchered, plucked, minced, stewed, and seasoned. We lack books without interpretation, books which contain facts rather than opinions. There are only a very few original writers, and the best differ from the others much less than would appear after superficial comparison. Some crawl, some limp, some dance, some run, some ride toward their goal, but the goal and the path are the same for all of them.

Great and original thoughts can be produced only in complete isolation, but how does one achieve isolation? One flees people— only to find oneself in the noisy marketplace of books. One can get rid of books, but how does one remove from one's head all the traditional knowledge that education has injected into it? In the art of becoming unlearned, true self-education is the most important, the most beautiful method, a method, however, which is hardly ever used—and almost always incompetently. Just as there are perhaps a thousand thinking men among a million, there is among a thousand thinkers only *one* self-reflective person. People today are like porridge; the one thing that gives them any form is the pot. Pithy and solid elements are found only on the scraper, in the lowest class of people. Most porridge is just porridge, and the spoon that scoops up a mouthful has not, by separating like elements, made them unlike.

True writing is not a Columbian journey of discovery, but rather an odyssey. Man is born in a foreign country; to live means to search for a homeland, and to think is to live. The motherland of thought is the heart, and he who yearns for a refreshing drink must dip into this fountain. The mind is nothing but a river; thousands have rested on its banks, and they muddy the water with washing, swimming, rinsing flax, and other mundane activities. The mind is the arm, the heart is the will. Strength can be developed; it can be increased and exercised. But what use is all this strength without the courage to employ it? An ignominious cowardice prevents all of us from thinking. More oppressive than the censorship of governments is the censorship exercised over our mind's work by public opinion. Most writers do not lack the intellect, but rather the character to be better than they are. Their weakness springs from vanity. The artist, the writer wants to tower above, to outdistance his contemporaries. But to tower above someone, you must stand next to him; to outdistance someone, you must travel the same road he does.

Good writers, therefore, have a lot in common with bad ones;

the good one contains the bad one. He is merely a bit more; he travels the road of the bad one, but he travels farther. He who heeds the voice of his own heart rather than the cries of the market-place, who has the courage to teach and propagate what his own heart has taught him, will always be original. Honesty is the source of genius, and man would be more inventive if he were more moral.

And now follows the practical advice I promised above. Take a few sheets of paper and for three consecutive days write down, without pretense or insincerity, everything that comes into your head. Write down what you think about yourself, about your lovers, the Turkish war, Goethe, Fonk's trial, the Last Judgment, your employers—and when the three days are over you will be beside yourself with astonishment at the unexpected, remarkable thoughts you have had. That is how to become an original writer in three days!

Index